A Year in the
Country

A Year in the
Country

ASSOCIATE CREATIVE DIRECTOR:
Christina Spalatin
DEPUTY EDITORS: Marija Andric,
Jennifer Zeigler
ART DIRECTOR: Scott Schiller
ASSOCIATE EDITOR: Julie Kuczynski
LAYOUT DESIGNERS: Joe Hrdina,
Chantell Singleton
COPY CHIEF: Deb Mulvey
CONTRIBUTING ART DIRECTOR:
Carole Ross
CONTRIBUTING LAYOUT DESIGNER:
Jennifer Ruetz
PRODUCTION ARTIST: Jill Banks
SENIOR RIGHTS ASSOCIATE: Jill Godsey

FRONT COVER: Sunflowers,
Thomas Nanos/Alamy Stock Photo

© 2019 RDA Enthusiast Brands, LLC.
1610 N. 2nd St., Suite 102
Milwaukee, WI 53212-3906

International Standard Book Number:
978-1-61765-842-6 (dated),
978-1-61765-843-3 (undated)
International Standard Serial Number:
2576-3679
Component Number:
116800021H (dated),
116800023H (undated)

TABLE OF CONTENTS

Welcome...

BECKY GRANT

Whether you live in or long for the country, paging through this awe-inspiring collection of moments and memories will satisfy your yearning for everything you love about rural life. *A Year in the Country* includes gorgeous photographs of sweeping landscapes and natural beauty, heartfelt stories, tried-and-true family recipes for special celebrations or everyday occasions, simple crafts to make for loved ones, and more. It's authentic from the first page to the last, because it comes from readers who contributed to *Country*, *Farm & Ranch Living*, *Country Woman* and *Birds & Blooms* magazines this past year.

The book is divided into four sections, one for each season, to make it easier for you to relish the best of the country all year long. No matter where you start reading, these favorites from the past year celebrate the best of the country spirit. And we promise the incredible photos of farms, animals and people will make you smile.

These personal, uplifting accounts celebrate country life, and they strike a chord in all our hearts.

We hope you savor this escape to the country.

—The Editors

Spring

These peach trees awaken in spring with a rainbow of blossoms at Lyman Orchards in Middlefield, Connecticut.
PHOTO BY TERRY WILD

THE GOOD LIFE

A Sliver of Heaven

Rolling up my sleeves and digging in the dirt on our Oregon farm is the life I dreamed of as a kid.

BY TAWNY NELSON *North Plains, Oregon*

Born in sunny state of California, I was an ocean-loving girl. However, when I was about 4 years old, my family uprooted and moved to Washington state, where for a short time we had the privilege of living one field over from where my maternal grandparents lived.

During those two years of my young life, the country grew roots in me deeper than the great depths of the ocean. The warm soil on my toes; the lush, green, rain-ripened grass fields; trees with great limbs for climbing; old red barns; and sweet carrots pulled fresh from the earth are just a few things that have never left my blood.

Three decades later, I finally get to live on my own piece of paradise on a little mountain in Oregon. My husband, Ben, and I farm hay on 80 acres, where we are raising our 20-month-old son, Michael, to be a true country kid.

Our home is located in the small town of North Plains, Oregon, near the Dixie Mountain Grange hall, in the middle of the Willamette and Tualatin valleys. This area has rich, fertile land where folks raise livestock and grow grass seed, hay, grapes and other fruit, pumpkins, nuts and Christmas trees. Multigeneration farms stand side by side with new ones.

After spending so many years in cities, I've had to learn how to farm and garden. Driving a tractor to cut, rake and bale hay was completely foreign to me. And, honestly, although Ben is a great teacher, it's still intimidating to work on such a large vehicle.

I always longed to grow my own vegetable garden like the one I used to raid at Grandma's, but I didn't know how. I have gotten guidance from Ben and my in-laws on how to plant seeds and fertilize, and on how much to water and when to stop watering—but there's also been a lot of Googling and trial and error. I'm still learning how to garden and how to can.

When it comes to flowers, I seem to have a black thumb (which I do intend to fix), but I'm in a constant state of euphoria when I roll up my sleeves and dig in

Tawny and Ben show their son, Michael, some outdoor fun—fishing on the Columbia River in Astoria, Oregon.

the earth, care for little chickens with my dog pals by my side, cook fresh-picked vegetables, walk along country lanes, ride four-wheelers all over the mountain or sit by a campfire.

Our house sits squarely in the middle of rolling hay fields that are surrounded by trees, secluding the fields from the outside world in their own little paradise. In our yard, Ben hung a swing from the shade-giving branches of a black walnut tree because of the swing I cherished at my grandparents' place as a child.

The elk meander in and out, sometimes only a few feet from our house. Bright daffodils and orchards give us a grand floral show each spring. I love the slight elevation

The Nelsons grow hay on 80 fertile acres that have been in the family for almost a century.

that can blanket us in snow in the winter, when the townsfolk usually only get rain.

I love our serene ponds, tucked into the swaying green fields, where a duck couple or two may decide to rest for the night.

I love the hand-built red barn, which looks beautiful in a blanket of dense fog; or shining in glory in the sunrise; or surrounded by the flaming yellows, oranges, reds and pinks of sunset; or covered in fresh white snow, set in the expanse of hay fields in contrast with the bright blue sky.

I love my in-laws' history with this place, which is nearing its century mark. Almost everything here was made and cherished by a previous generation. My husband's paternal grandfather bought this land in 1945 from the original homesteaders. They then cleared the fields of old-growth timber by hand. Ben's dad remembers his father dynamiting each and every

Michael and his buddy, Elsa, peek into the barn to spy on the chickens.

The country grew roots in me deeper than the great depths of the ocean.

stump, afterward smoothing the dirt for hay and, at one time, also for strawberries.

I love the rickety old shack where pigs were bred, the barn's milking stations, and the machine shop.

I love the dip in our lawn where the farm's original dirt-floor house used to stand. I love the newer, not-dirt-floor house built in the '50s that Ben and I renovated together to make our own.

And I love that our son gets to grow up here, Lord willing, as the next generation to enjoy the beauty of creation, learning the values of hard but satisfying work, the faith and patience it takes to wait for crops to grow, the compassion and care for neighbors and little animals, and the reward in feeding and helping those around us. This truly is a piece of heaven, and we are blessed to enjoy it together. ☀

Elk often graze a few feet from Tawny's home.

Special Delivery!

There are surprises around every turn as a rural mail carrier.

BY MELINDA HAGER *Martin, Kentucky*

For the past 33 years, I have delivered mail in eastern Kentucky. I started straight out of high school, and I think it's a wonderful job. Each day is memorable.

I look forward to seeing friendly faces along my route. There's a myth that dogs and mail carriers don't get along, but the doggies on my route love me. One dog, named Bandit, meets me at the gate with his toy almost every day. I take a few moments out of my busy schedule to play fetch with him.

If a dog is missing, I keep a lookout. I've even taken a few back to their owners. The best rescue has to be Woogie. I'm not sure how he got lost, but he recognized my car, so I held my door open and told him to get in if he wanted to go home.

With no hesitation, Woogie, a Chihuahua, jumped into my car and onto my husband's lap, and off we went. When I pulled into the driveway, his owner's grandkids yelled, "Hey, look! Woogie is in the mail car!"

Delivering mail in the country has challenges, too. Weather can be a big factor, especially in the winter, but the animals are where the real difficulties come

Melinda looks forward to seeing friendly faces, like Woogie, on her mail route.

from, like having to watch out for chickens running loose everywhere.

In one holler, I have to fight with the horses to reach the mailboxes. They can be very stubborn, so I try to inch forward with my car and gently encourage them to move out of the way.

When I first started, my Uncle Otis would wait for me at his mailbox. He'd ask me to help herd cattle from one side of the road to the other. So I'd park my car as a barrier and we would walk them across to the other pasture.

One morning I spotted a mother duck and her babies trying to cross. I flashed my lights and slowed the other drivers down so the birds could safely make it across.

During summer, I get vegetables from the garden. During Christmas, I get candy, pumpkin rolls and nut breads. One customer leaves me a little something when he takes a notion to bake. I truly love these surprises.

The people on my route are some of the best in the world. When someone is out in their yard, I greet them with a smile and a hello. They are more like family than customers, and I'm proud to do my part to help the community. ☀

Dick skins logs for the cabin in early spring, when they peel more easily; stuck in the mud with 7 miles to go.

Spring Breakup in Kenai

Over the hills and through the mud, my family raced against the clock to start our new life in the Alaskan wild.

BY DICK SCHULLER *Goldendale, Washington*

Our World War II Dodge Power Wagon truck sank again; stuck for the sixth time. A flurry of doubt flashed across my mind. Why was I dragging my wife, Dot, and three small children 7 miles back into the uncharted countryside? The reason: Homesteading 160 acres, only $1.25 per acre. This was a great deal, even back in 1959.

Our friend Bernie backed up his ancient truck, fitted with huge DC-3 airplane tires. He smiled and quipped, "If I get stuck, we'll really be in trouble."

Mud flailed into the air as the chained-up vehicle slowly lurched forward. Why didn't we wait until spring—called breakup time on the Kenai Peninsula—passed and just drive in on solid, dry ground? Why pick the worst time of the year?

Our deadline for occupying the land was in two days. If we missed it, others wanting to file on our land would be at the Anchorage government land office waiting to counterclaim; we'd be out.

At least the Kenai area was bathed in sunshine, the days were long, and summer mosquitoes were still asleep.

Bernie and I had been coming to the homestead on weekends. We had constructed a 10-by-10-foot temporary cabin until we could build a log house.

Dot was generally resilient and took problems with a smile. But she had emphatically stated, "We've got to have the log house finished before winter. I am not spending an Alaskan winter in a hundred square feet cabin with three young children. I am not!"

After a quick lurch along the trail, we churned on, dreading the steepest hill on the entire trail. Skidding back and forth from the previous ruts, I gained the top. Our son, Rick, and daughters, Linda and Annette, piled out and started laughing convulsively. When I looked at my now empty truck, I saw the humor.

Yes, we had roared up the rutted hill, but our belongings were strewn in the oozing mud. There, upended, was the old white cookstove; beyond were our bed frame, dishes and a case of peas.

Since we couldn't turn around for fear of getting stuck again, we carried necessary objects back to the truck. We decided to leave some heavier things behind and come back when they dried out.

We had already traveled 15 gravel miles from the small fishing village of Kenai. The job at hand was to reach our homestead before dark.

At 8:30 p.m. we were still jumping out of the trucks and throwing things back on. Soon we had only 1mile to reach the homestead, and we had to go up another steep hill. We retied our loads again. The truck engines were tired and overheated.

Bernie spoke words of wisdom. "It's getting dark and we won't make it if we get stuck again. Why not jump on my truck and ride it to the homestead? We can come back in the morning."

Dot and I agreed as we lifted the exhausted children into the cab and the two of us crawled onto the back and hung on tenaciously.

Our little shack was inviting as we spotted it in the evening twilight. Dot and I stumbled around trying to make sandwiches for a quick supper and fix the cabin for sleeping. Annette, our 3-year-old, was cradled in Dot's arms. She awoke and asked, "Mom, where is the bathroom?" We had yet to build an outhouse.

The next morning all of us adults greeted achy muscles we didn't know we had. I did my best to help make Dot and the kids comfortable. Bernie was homesteading 2 miles away, and he could look in on my family until we got more established.

Getting here sure wasn't easy, but the land was ours! I thanked the Lord for his help in making the dream of a lifetime possible. ☀

The family's log house, which took five months to build; Dot washes clothes with her "Alaska Maytag"; Rick and Linda float down the lake on a rustic raft.

A Dream in Progress

Now that we finally have our own land, the possibilities seem endless.

BY ARANDA VANCE *Richlands, Virginia*

The search was long but the land was worth the wait. James, Luke, Logan and Aranda love the country.

Wanting land is a desire I've had longer than I can even remember. Luckily, I married someone like-minded. My husband, James, is the son of a pastor whose family of 10 rented an old farmhouse and occasionally worked on the farm.

James fell in love with the land as a 4-year-old boy, playing in the creek, chasing cows, picking beans and sitting in a tree while eating ripe mulberries.

As for me, I ran wild outside at my grandparents' house. They gardened a lot, kept bees and had fruit trees. There was a pond for fishing and dipping, plus plenty of room to just be a kid full of imagination. I remember picking up the potatoes as my grandfather dug them and then letting the dirt run through my fingers.

Married life, college and work made me doubt the likelihood of my farming dream coming true. But when our firstborn made his appearance after 10 years of marriage and two miscarriages, we wanted to give

him the moon. To us, that meant land, so our "someday" would have to start right then.

Selling our house took years. But once it sold, browsing for property turned into looking in earnest. We were flexible on many factors, and our radius was large. Still, our first year of searching ended with no purchase.

In the second year, we made an offer that was refused. And we discovered that decent land was not only hard to come by, but exorbitant in price.

After seeing the cost of several promising properties, James and I would joke, "There's gold in them there hills!"

Year three of searching yielded our second miracle: Now we had two boys who'd need wide-open spaces, trees and work to keep them busy as they got older.

We learned that a lot of the land here is in heirship; in some cases, multiple people had inherited part of a single property, making things complicated, to say the least.

We looked at beautiful land, and we looked at land that wasn't perfect. Nothing panned out.

Two little helpers and Dad stack wood to rebuild the barn; James plants the first mulberry tree on the farm.

We've worked hard to make the land usable… In the process, we've fallen in love with our piece of ground all the more.

Then one ordinary day, we learned that a property we'd passed on in nearby Russell County because of size had been combined with an adjacent lot. We went to look at it as a family, then signed a contract a few days later.

I expected something to fall through, so imagine my surprise when we (along with the bank) became the owners!

We've worked hard to make the land usable, and we've played quite a bit, too. In the process, we've fallen in love with our piece of ground all the more.

There's a stream where the boys can race their imaginary boats. On hot summer days after work, we splash in the water together. We've picked berries, had bonfires, gone four-wheeling, hiked, hunted and watched sunsets. With help from their dad, the boys have built roads for their dump trucks.

They've relished getting dirty, learning about trees and animals and picnicking on the grass. I have thousands of snapshots in my mind of the memories we'll make here.

While we don't live on the land yet, we have a camper that we'll be moving there when the weather gets warmer. Our foundation is finished and we plan to have our home under a roof by summer's end. That will be a good thing, too, because it gets harder to leave every time. Logan, our 5-year-old, says, "I can't wait to live here all the time." Younger brother Luke cries if he can't go to the land they are ready to call home.

We're planning for livestock. There are places for chickens and pigs, goats and sheep, and a few cows. We've cleared overgrown pasture and planted 600 trees, not to mention wildflowers.

We've taken rock from the areas we're improving and lined over 1,000 feet of ditch. Every rock has been touched by me, James, Logan or Luke. We've torn down a barn from a Tennessee farm that was subdivided, and now we're in the process of rebuilding it here.

Most importantly, there's room for two little boys to grow up playing with rocks and dirt and picking mulberries. We can make it our bit of heaven. As we were planting some fruit trees the other day, I let the dirt run through my fingers and couldn't help but laugh. After an almost five-year journey, we have our own dirt!

It's wholesome, honest work with honest results. At the end of a day or a month or a even a year, you can stand back and say, "We did this." Still, what I love best about building our farm is the time it allows us to spend together, grow together and create something special that will last. I can't think of any hobby, career or anything else that provides a family the quality time this life has given us. For that, I am most grateful.

We say the land is ours. But after all the time spent working, walking and enjoying it, we have found that we belong to the land just as much as it belongs to us. ☀

Ember Evans (with her dad, Cory) watches her grandpa Steven Yettaw boil sap to make maple syrup.

First Harvest of Spring

A delightful sweetness awaits with this yearly syruping tradition.

BY JESSICA EVANS *Harbor Springs, Michigan*

Vermont is usually what comes to mind when people think about maple syrup. However, in the hills of northern Michigan, maple trees abound, and there are many folks who head out to the sugarbush to tap trees each spring. My family is among them.

In early March, Dad shovels out his "sap shack" to get ready for the impending start of the sweet stuff. As a child, I always loved maple syrup season because it meant longer days outside enjoying 45-degree weather (practically tropical after a long, snowy winter) and gathering buckets full of sap.

My folks always made it fun. While the sap boiled down into a delicious syrup, we had a cookout. Mom made potato salad and baked beans, and we roasted hot dogs on the fire, with s'mores for dessert.

I moved away after college, but five years ago, my husband, Cory, and I decided to return home to northern Michigan. Our daughter, Ember, was born in March 2016—a lucky month, I think! The following spring, she helped her daddy and grandpa make maple syrup for the first time. I am blessed to see her savor the sweetness of spring with her grandparents just like I did as a child. ☀

The Day I Saved Twizzler the Duck

Feathered friend teaches this country vet that the job comes with surprises.

BY ERIKA EIGENBROD *Lincoln, Illinois*

When I was in veterinary school, I had an idealistic view of my future. I would balance home life and work, emergencies would have quick fixes, and I'd be prepared for every call. There'd be no surprises. Well, I can tell you reality is much different.

One such surprise came while I was on call for my rural clinic. My husband and I were home debating who would bathe our son when the phone rang. The voice on the other end said, "Hello, doctor? We have a client on the phone with a very lethargic duck."

While the phone was ringing to the client, I wondered if I had the wrong animal. A duck emergency? Talking with the owner, it became clear that Twizzler, a jumbo Pekin, was in distress.

I racked my brain for anything I'd learned in school about ducks. Panicking, I called a colleague for advice, which he graciously gave.

On arrival, Twizzler was alert but had some difficulty standing and breathing. Her owners gave me the full story, saying they had noticed her limping but that she'd seemed OK—and, no, she hadn't laid an egg this week.

I gave Twizzler medications for pain and some fluids, but nothing relaxed her. I suggested we take a radiograph to make sure she was not egg bound. The picture showed it: a very large, diagonally situated egg. She also had a fracture in her left femur. After explaining this to the owners, I had to get the egg out.

I tried manual removal with no luck. I gave her calcium and used warm water and fluid bags to try to help the muscles contract. After spending a considerable amount of time in Twizzler's tail end, I was running out of options and she was becoming more distressed.

A colleague suggested anesthesia. I explained the risks to the owners, and to the surgery room we went. With Twizzler relaxed at last, I tried again to extract the egg. After a few tries, I touched the shell; soon, the egg was out. What a relief!

Once she was awake, Twizzler started to act normal. The next 24 to 48 hours would be crucial for her, but she seemed to be on the right track.

Being a veterinarian has taught me to embrace the unexpected. Never did I imagine that I'd be called for an emergency egg extraction on a duck named Twizzler, but the human-animal bond is amazing. Twizzler's family truly loves their duck. ☀

Erika is all smiles after helping Twizzler through her troubles; the X-ray below shows the misaligned egg.

CAPTURE THE BEAUTY AROUND YOU

SCRAPBOOK

I felt such joy, peace and awe as I admired these tulip fields in
La Conner, Washington. This just has to be what heaven will be like!
ANNETTE ARCHULETA *Spokane, Washington*

Snowcap lives on a local farm, and I'm sure he was happy to have
a pasture full of spring grass and dandelions to munch on.
CAROLYN ANDERSON *New Alexandria, Pennsylvania*

Anyone who knew my Grandma Bernice knew she loved birds and that her favorite was the mountain bluebird. I think of my grandma every time I see one of these birds, especially in spring.
BRENDA KERTTU *Naples, Idaho*

Muddy toddler Titus watches Daddy on the tractor. He is studying every move so that he can drive it one day, too.
KIRSTIN CARLSON *Elk Point, South Dakota*

Patty T. Pig, my 1,000-pound pet, passed away at 16. Patty played a large role in the community and children adored her.
JAMIE CRUZ *Littleton, Massachusetts*

Spring storms not only bring flowers, but rainbows, too!
LOU ANN RUGG
Mill Run, Pennsylvania

Preparation Canyon in the Loess Hills is spectacular anytime,
but you definitely don't want to miss it during spring.
RACHEL SWENSEN *Harlan, Iowa*

One of our newly hatched baby chicks peeks out from
under Momma's feathers. It is hard to believe
there are nine more underneath her!
RACHEL CLELLAND *Lake Norden, South Dakota*

Just as my daughter, Trinity, made a wish
(for a unicorn), a breeze blew the
dandelion seeds back at her.
SHAYE COBB *Blairsville, Georgia*

Cooper, our Labrador retriever, sat in the back of our '52 Chevy enjoying the sunshine when I took this photo on a chilly morning. He may not look too impressed—he's used to me taking pictures of him. Cooper is a farm dog and loves to ride in the truck.
ASHLEY FORD *Hamilton, Missouri*

The early morning light in Schwabacher Landing gives me a feeling of peace. I often revisit the memory of taking this photo in Grand Teton National Park in Wyoming. The view is a gift from above for us mortals.
DANA FOREMAN *Old Fort, North Carolina*

Every spring and throughout most of the year, 50 to 100 hummingbirds, like this male Calliope, visit my 11 feeders. They drink about 2 gallons of sugar water per day! April is my favorite month because I've had as many as six species show up then—Anna's, rufous, Calliope, black-chinned, Allen's and a single Costa's.
ELIJAH GILDEA *Redding, California*

My grandchildren race back to the barn on their horses after a long day spent rounding up cattle. Grace leads the way on Vegas, followed by Lexi on Ruby and Mac on Bugsy. My heart swells with pride while watching these kids live the country life.
SUZANN MILLER *Hyrum, Utah*

My husband, Matt, and 2-year-old son, Charlie, are the sixth and, hopefully, seventh generations to work this cornfield. The land is our future.
HILARY KOLLASCH *Whittemore, Iowa*

My granddaughters take their mini John Deere Gator out on our family's 4-acre sesquicentennial farm. Kennedy, 4, drives while 2-year-old Kassidy holds on.
CAROLYN ALLEN *Springport, Michigan*

This corncrib is tucked away on an old homeplace not far from where I live. I pass by every day, and I had to stop and take a picture of this gorgeous tree.
DONNA JOHNSON *Woodlawn, Virginia*

We're new at farming, but our boy Greyson already found a pal to share secrets with.
McKELL GROOTERS *Fremont, Michigan*

Clyde, our rescue pup, quickly bonded with our daughter Israella. It was love at first sight, and now the two of them are seldom apart. There sure is a lot of laughter in our home!
CATHY CONDER *Freeport, Illinois*

A lamb sidles up to this ewe for a springtime snapshot exemplifying renewed life.
PHOTO BY RACHEL WRIGHT

I was in New Mexico taking photos of wild horses when I came upon a small herd of mustangs grazing on the open range. As I got a little closer, I captured this loving shot of the stallion and his mares. Having the opportunity to be out in nature, moving among this herd of animals, is an experience I will never forget.
JERRY COWART *Chatsworth, California*

Mount Mansfield, the highest peak in Vermont, still harbors winter's chill above the Pleasant Valley below it. Here, along a 10-mile road between Cambridge and Underhill, spring green begins its battle with the snow.
PHOTO BY JOHN H. KNOX

Cardinals visit my yard every day year-round. During the spring, they often perch in my blooming crabapple tree. I love this time of year.
REBECCA GRANGER *Bancroft, Michigan*

I drove to Burlington, Washington, on a March day. A friend had given me a tip on this beautiful Dutch gambrel barn that was built in the late 1930s.
JEFF SCHENEKL *Arlington, Washington*

This International Harvester tractor has been in the family for years.
I snapped this picture when I was at the barn as the sun set.
REBECCA FINCHUM *Strawberry Plains, Tennessee*

These pretty crocuses were my grandmother's flowers. I always look forward
to their arrival at the end of winter.
AMANDA KRISTULA
Mifflintown, Pennsylvania

My son Shepard is living up to his name and
bonding with the babies on our family farm.
KAYLA McDERMITT *Carrollton, Georgia*

**Moving from the city to the country with our children has been
such a blessing. It's a slower, sweeter life and we adore it.**
RENDI TRENT *Oakdale, California*

HEART & SOUL

Chicken Therapy for the Spirit

The hens in this yard bring their keeper to a place of peace and reflection.

BY BECKY SERNETTT *Cazenovia, New York*

In Japan, a walk through the woods is also known as forest bathing, which refers to the therapeutic practice of taking in the sights, smells and sounds of the wilderness. In essence, the hiker is bathing in the woods. This activity, as many a lover of the outdoors can attest, offers immune-boosting and stress-relieving benefits.

On my homestead in central New York, we engage in chicken bathing. This does not mean giving our feathered friends a good washing. It's our name for time spent with the Brahmas, Buff Orpingtons, Ameraucanas, Barred Plymouth Rocks and Rhode Island Reds. The chickens' fenced-in yard provides plenty of room for them to roam, with a few chairs for humans to sit and offer treats or take in the sights, smells and sounds.

For there's something about spending time with chickens in their natural environment that soothes the soul. Perhaps it is their quirky personalities, how one chicken's call can stand out. (Our loudest hen is named Jellybean.) Or maybe it's how they follow behind us like ducklings, how leading them across the grass can make one feel as important as Moses guiding his flock.

Their confounding dumbness is endearing, too: the way they plop down at night, one hen atop another, on a ramp leading to a closed coop door, when only 2 feet away another door is wide open. And there's the obvious: their miraculous daily eggs.

All of these qualities are part of the chicken charm, but there's something else, something that leads me to promise you this: Spend just 15 minutes "bathing" in

For Becky Sernett and her daughter, Amanda, hanging out with hens like Lily, a Light Brahma (above), is great therapy.

Time spent with hens, such as this Silver Laced Wyandotte, can put anyone at ease.

Spend just 15 minutes "bathing" in the yard, and you'll experience moments of wonder.

the yard, and you'll experience moments of wonder. Our docile Buff Orpington, Sunny, may be foraging through the weeds, her fluffy blond-feathered butt in the air, and in an instant, she's chasing a wren from her territory like a velociraptor after its prey. Look deep into chickens' yellow eyes, observe their scaly clawed feet, and you, too, will believe they descended from dinosaurs. Fall asleep in their yard, and they might peck you to death, in their innocent, being-a-chicken way.

And so maybe this feathered contradiction of domestication and wildness is what draws the chicken lover to spend just a few extra minutes in the yard. No one in the know will question you when you say you're going out to check the chickens and you're gone for an hour, or two, or more!

There's no age restriction for chicken bathing. In sixth grade, my daughter wrote an essay about our chickens to document a year spent experiencing their wonder. All you need are a few hens and space for them to be their natural chicken selves, and you have access to some of the best therapy in the world. ☀

Whisper will always be
a winner in Paige's heart.

Back on Track

*My horse Whisper and I leaned on
each other for support in hard times.*

BY PAIGE CERULLI *Plainfield, Massachusetts*

When I was in college, I met Whisper. A young thoroughbred, she was a bit spooky and a lot green. A year later, I was in a major car accident, suffering a traumatic brain injury that would change my life. I battled dizziness, memory loss, sensitivity to light and sound, and migraines—and that's just the short list of the troubles.

Doctors told me that another head injury would be catastrophic, and a fall from a horse was a risk I should not take. An ex-racehorse wasn't the ideal match for me, but when I rode Whisper a few months later, she was quieter and dependable. Instead of spooking at invisible monsters or trying to break into a trot or canter, she walked quietly as I relearned how to balance.

It wasn't the last time Whisper walked me through tough times. I purchased her a year to the day after my accident, and she became my very first horse.

After graduating with a double major in English and flute performance, I learned I had a medical condition and injuries that would end my music career. This was devastating; I'd sacrificed so much for my future, and it was taken from me before it began.

I turned to Whisper. Riding her took considerable concentration, so it was the only activity that kept me from agonizing over what I'd lost. And Whisper was there when I needed to sit in the pasture and think.

We had countless adventures together. We went for rides in the snow and learned equine agility. We even took part in an episode of *Horse Master* with Julie Goodnight. Julie taught me more about riding than I'd learned in years of lessons. Whisper was injury-prone, so I also learned about equine rehabilitation and first aid.

Last fall, I bought a house with a small barn and brought Whisper home with me. She had to be fully retired at 16 because of medical issues, but she's now teaching Lyric, a younger ex-racehorse, about good manners and behavior.

I know I won't have Whisper forever, so I appreciate every day. On paper, she may not have been the right horse for me, but life sometimes gives us exactly what we need. Thank goodness I love thoroughbreds. ☀

The First Song of Spring

Peepers herald the new life that warmer weather and longer days bring.

BY MARLENE SMITH *Homer, New York*

What would spring be like without peepers? Sadly, I know. I've lived in peeperless places. But here, the tiny frogs have an almost mystical presence. I've been told some people have spring rituals, searching for the first ones.

When you live near water, as I do, they're the first thing you hear on a spring morning and the last thing you hear at night. Folks I know who live near a marsh say the peeping gets so overwhelming that they have to keep the windows closed—but still they lose sleep. My creek is far enough away that I don't have that problem. I love the sound of the water, whether it's a gentle gurgle or the steady roar after a heavy rain. It's even better if there's an amphibian chorus to go with it.

The frogs ignite my curiosity. I've never seen one, though, because their song stops whenever I draw near. Perhaps they do it to protect themselves from predators, but what if it's really because they're talking about us and don't want us to overhear?

I'm surprised they manage to be heard over a roaring creek after a spring thaw. I've heard they peep to attract their mates, but I'm not convinced. I think it's a calculated attempt to get people to quiet down and listen.

Kidding aside, trying to tune out their call is like closing the curtains on the springtime sun. If you are tempted to Google their sound, I'd recommend not wasting your time. It wouldn't do them justice any more than eating one potato chip satisfies a craving. It's best, if you can, to listen to the real thing on a beautiful spring night. I even look forward to a part of my commute because I can lower my window and be serenaded on the way to work and again on the trip home.

I grew up to the sweet sound of peepers, but life took me to other cities and another country. One evening when I was toying with the idea of moving back to where I grew up, I was on the phone with someone from home. I could hear the siren's song in the background, and that tipped the scales.

I wanted to live again where I could hear them. I moved and have been here happily ever since. John Muir wrote, "The mountains are calling and I must go." For me, it was the call of the peepers. ☀

> These frogs hibernate all winter until the thaw signals it's time for their familiar tune.

Kevin sits 48 feet up, atop a grain bin surrounded by flooded fields.

The Great Grain Rescue

*When floodwaters threatened a farm's harvest,
dozens donated their time and trucks to help out.*

BY KEVIN WEITKAMP *Pocohontas, Arkansas*

On May 3, 2017, Pocahontas, Arkansas, was hit by historical flooding. The Black River reached levels never before seen, threatening to blow through a levee that was protecting thousands of acres of farmland.

I am the co-operator of Weitkamp Farms, which stood in the direct path of the overflowing levee. After realizing the barrier wasn't going to hold the water back, we were faced with the possibility that the 56,000 bushels of rice, corn and soybeans left in our grain bins would be lost to flooding.

We started trucking grain out on May 2 at 7 a.m., knowing that without assistance there wasn't a chance of getting it all out. However, our prayer was answered when friends and neighbors started pouring in to help us.

With everyone giving it their all, we moved the 56,000 bushels in 28 straight hours of work. We finished at noon on May 3. The levee breached that afternoon.

Hundreds of acres of planted cropland flooded, but at least our grain in the bins was saved, thanks to many kind folks who went above and beyond to help in our time of need. ☀

Keeping Mom Close

A mother's heirloom charm bracelet becomes necklaces for her daughters.

BY JEANNE AMBROSE *Milwaukee, Wisconsin*

My mother gave me her charm bracelet years before she died, but I never wore it. I'm just not a bracelet person. It stayed tucked in my jewelry box, cherished but hidden. When a friend wrote a book called *The Charm Bracelet*, I was inspired to pull out my mother's tarnished silver heirloom from its hiding spot. And I decided I wanted to share it with my five sisters.

Instead of mailing the bracelet from state to state in a sort of time-share arrangement (which we'd once done with a treasured family quilt), I decided to use the charms to create necklaces. Each of my sisters (sorry, big brother) got one as a gift from me as a memento of Mom.

Although I could have done the project myself, I have a friend whose hobby is jewelry-making. Better to hand it off to someone who has drawers full of beads and clasps and chains.

She and I talked about my sisters: Marcia, Sandy, Cathy, Mary and Terri. What are their birthstones and styles? Silver or gold? Simple or embellished? We figured out the appropriate personality for each necklace and divvied up the charms, some with a significance that still remains a mystery to me.

The baby shoes probably were a gift to my mom when Marcia, her first child, was born. There was a mini bowling alley with a teensy moveable ball that could be "rolled" down the alley to knock over tiny pins. That would be perfect for Mary, whose son once worked at a bowling alley. There was an old-time wringer washing machine charm. A tiny wedding ring. An old-fashioned stand mixer that had moving parts. A religious symbol. A medal for her completion of a Dorothy Carnegie course. There were entwined hearts engraved with the words "you/me."

Those charms—once hidden away in my jewelry box—have been brought back to life for my sisters, who now wear them close to their hearts. ☀

Clockwise from left are Mary with her doll, Marcia, father Louis Schulz, Sandy, Cathy, Terri, Mike and mother Catherine Schulz holding Jeanne.

Rolled with Love

Making sweet memories baking pies in Mama's country kitchen.

BY CONNIE THOMPSON *Blackfoot, Idaho*

Mama, like many women of the 1950s, was a wonderful cook. Every dish and dessert she made was delicious, but to her family, nothing brought more anticipation than her pies.

The crust was always flaky with just the right amount of crisp.

I asked Mama, "What makes your pies taste so good?" Her gracious reply was always the same: "The secret is in the crust. Each one has a lot of love rolled into it."

As a girl, I climbed onto a stool and peered at the counter freshly dusted with flour. "What kind are we making this week?" I asked. Like a doctor with his tools laid before him, my mother would prepare to bake. Pie pans, check. Pastry blender, check. But the tool that I fancied most was her wooden rolling pin.

Mama always saved the dough trimmings for me to make my own pies. I adored the way the rolling pin felt in my tiny hands. And the aroma of cinnamon teased my taste buds while my special pies baked in the oven.

Connie's mother, Carole, passed her values and baking skills to the next generation.

The filling came from our garden, which was a magical place that yielded wonderful gifts for our pie-making adventures.

Fresh rhubarb in spring was followed by lip-smacking summer berries picked straight from the vine. Peaches in the summer faded to apples in the fall, and winter brought pumpkin spice.

As an adult, I appreciate the life lessons I learned in that country garden and in Mama's kitchen. The value of hard work and a job well done are two that come to mind.

Mama always said, "Anything worth having is worth working for." You know what? Mama was right about that.

On my 40th birthday, Mama surprised me with the coveted rolling pin.

Tucked between a few layers of brightly colored tissue paper and a ribbon was a note: "Look back and think of me for just a moment each time you pull this rolling pin from the shelf. Then look forward to new memories you will make with your own daughters. May they be as sweet as ours." ☀

Driven to Success

As a saleswoman in the 1930s, Grandma brought home more than just the bacon.

BY CANDACE WILBER HORCH *Woodinville, Washington*

Candace Wilber Horch bought this 1931 Ford Model A (top) because it was just like the one her grandmother drove on sales calls (bottom). Grandma Grace's door-to-door sales job helped her family's farm stay afloat.

During the Great Depression, my grandmother Grace Mills Wilber sold Wilknit hosiery door to door in Dallas County, Iowa. It was a tough time, and she sought to earn supplementary income to support her two young sons and to help her farmer husband make ends meet.

She was such a skilled saleswoman that, in 1931, the Wilknit Hoisery Co. awarded her a brand-new car, a 1931 Ford Model A. That dependable automobile became her work "truck," and she used it to haul in a bounty of additional money for her family. Eventually, my grandmother's work ethic earned her three more cars.

Recently, I saw a 1931 Ford Model A for sale on a lot in a small town nearby. I bought it in memory of Grandma Grace. Everything about the car is original, and I do not plan to update it.

On a wall in my house hang two framed pictures that I treasure. One shows my grandmother standing beside the Model A, sales case in hand, ready to go out on a call. In that photo, a farm chicken hurries past the front of the vehicle. In the other, I tried to re-create Grandma Grace's photo, minus the chicken.

I also have one of the small ledgers that she used to record her orders and the black case in which she carried her hosiery samples.

Grandma Grace died when I was 5. Now, 87 years after she earned her first car, I love having these reminders that keep her close to me. ☀

Dijon-Rubbed Pork with Rhubarb Sauce

PREP: 15 min. • **BAKE:** 1 hour + standing
MAKES: 12 servings (1½ cups sauce)

- 1 **boneless pork loin roast (3 lbs.)**
- ¼ **cup Dijon mustard**
- 6 **garlic cloves, minced**
- 1 **Tbsp. minced fresh rosemary or 1 tsp. dried rosemary, crushed**
- ¾ **tsp. salt**
- ½ **tsp. pepper**

SAUCE
- 3 **cups sliced fresh or frozen rhubarb**
- ⅓ **cup orange juice**
- ⅓ **cup sugar**
- 1 **Tbsp. cider vinegar**

1. Score the surface of the pork, making diamond shapes ¼ in. deep. In a small bowl, combine the mustard, garlic, rosemary, salt and pepper; rub over pork.
2. Coat a roasting pan and rack with cooking spray; place pork on rack in the pan. Bake, uncovered, at 350° until a thermometer reads 145°, about 1 hour. Let stand for 10 minutes before slicing.
3. In a small saucepan, bring the sauce ingredients to a boil. Reduce heat; cover and simmer until rhubarb is tender, 8-12 minutes. Serve warm with pork.
NOTE If using frozen rhubarb, measure rhubarb while still frozen, then thaw completely. Drain in a colander, but do not press liquid out.

3 oz. cooked pork and 2 Tbsp. sauce: 181 cal., 6g fat (2g sat. fat), 56mg chol., 308mg sod., 9g carb. (7g sugars, 1g fiber), 23g pro.
Diabetic exchanges: 3 lean meat, ½ starch.

Dad's Blueberry Buttermilk Pancakes

PREP: 15 min. + standing • **COOK:** 10 min./batch
MAKES: 12 pancakes

- 1 cup all-purpose flour
- 3 Tbsp. cornmeal
- 3 Tbsp. quick-cooking oats
- 3 Tbsp. sugar
- 1 tsp. baking powder
- ½ tsp. baking soda
- ½ tsp. salt
  Dash ground nutmeg
- 1 large egg
- 1½ cups buttermilk
- 2 Tbsp. canola oil
- 1 tsp. vanilla extract
- 1 cup fresh or frozen blueberries

1. In a large bowl, whisk the first eight ingredients. In another bowl, whisk egg, buttermilk, oil and vanilla until blended. Add to flour mixture; stir just until moistened (batter will be lumpy). Let stand 15 minutes.
2. Lightly grease a griddle or large nonstick skillet; heat over medium heat. Stir blueberries into batter. Pour batter by ¼ cupfuls onto griddle or skillet. Cook until bubbles on top begin to pop and bottoms are golden brown. Turn; cook until second side is brown.

3 pancakes: 332 cal., 10g fat (2g sat. fat), 50mg chol., 746mg sod., 52g carb. (18g sugars, 2g fiber), 9g pro.

Hot Spinach Apple Salad

TAKES: 20 min. • **MAKES:** 10 servings

- 6 bacon strips, diced
- ¼ cup cider vinegar
- 3 Tbsp. brown sugar
- 9 cups fresh baby spinach
- 2 unpeeled large red apples, thinly sliced
- 1 medium red onion, chopped (about ¾ cup)

1. In a large skillet, cook bacon until crisp. Remove to paper towels. Drain, reserving 2 Tbsp. drippings.
2. In same skillet, combine vinegar, brown sugar and reserved drippings. Bring to a boil; cook and stir until sugar is dissolved. Cool slightly.
3. Meanwhile, in a serving bowl, combine spinach, apples, onion and bacon. Drizzle with warm dressing; toss to coat. Serve immediately.

1 serving: 117 cal., 7g fat (2g sat. fat), 11mg chol., 135mg sod., 11g carb. (9g sugars, 2g fiber), 3g pro.
Diabetic exchanges: 1 vegetable, 1 fat, ½ starch.

Fruity Croissant Puff

PREP: 10 min. + chilling • **BAKE:** 45 min. • **MAKES:** 6 servings

- 4 large croissants, cut into 1-in. cubes (about 6 cups)
- 1½ cups mixed fresh berries
- 1 pkg. (8 oz.) cream cheese, softened
- 1 cup 2% milk
- ½ cup sugar
- 2 large eggs
- 1 tsp. vanilla extract
  Maple syrup, optional

1. Place croissants and berries in a greased 8-in. square baking dish. In a medium bowl, beat cream cheese until smooth. Beat in milk, sugar, eggs and vanilla until blended; pour over croissants. Refrigerate, covered, overnight.

2. Preheat oven to 350°. Remove casserole from refrigerator while oven heats.

3. Bake, covered, 30 minutes. Bake, uncovered, until puffed and golden and a knife inserted in the center comes out clean, 15-20 minutes. Let stand 5-10 minutes before serving. If desired, serve with syrup.

1 serving: 429 cal., 24g fat (14g sat. fat), 132mg chol., 358mg sod., 44g carb. (27g sugars, 2g fiber), 9g pro.

Broccoli Mac & Cheese Bake

PREP: 25 min. • **BAKE:** 20 min. • **MAKES:** 12 servings

- 3 cups uncooked elbow macaroni
- 4 cups fresh broccoli florets
- ½ cup butter, cubed
- 3 Tbsp. all-purpose flour
- ½ tsp. garlic powder
- ½ tsp. onion powder
- ¼ tsp. pepper
- ⅛ tsp. salt
- 2 cans (12 oz. each) evaporated milk
- 2½ cups shredded cheddar cheese, divided
- ½ cup crushed cornbread-flavored crackers (about 6 crackers)

1. Cook macaroni according to package directions, adding broccoli during the last 3-4 minutes; drain.

2. In a large saucepan, melt butter. Stir in the flour, garlic powder, onion powder, pepper and salt until smooth; gradually stir in evaporated milk. Bring to a boil; cook and stir until thickened, about 2 minutes. Remove from the heat; stir in 2 cups cheese.

3. Place half of macaroni and broccoli in a greased 13x9-in. baking dish. Top with half of the cheese sauce. Repeat layers. Sprinkle with cracker crumbs and remaining cheese.

4. Bake, uncovered, at 375° until bubbly, 20-25 minutes.

¾ cup: 335 cal., 21g fat (12g sat. fat), 61mg chol., 331mg sod., 25g carb. (7g sugars, 1g fiber), 13g pro.

Brunch Hash & Egg Bake

PREP: 45 min. • **BAKE:** 15 min.
MAKES: 8 servings

2   lbs. Yukon Gold potatoes, peeled and cut into ¾-in. pieces
1   lb. bulk Italian sausage
1   large onion, finely chopped
¼   cup olive oil
¼   tsp. salt
¼   tsp. pepper
8   large eggs
1   cup crumbled feta cheese
    Minced fresh parsley

1. Preheat oven to 375°. Place potatoes in a large saucepan; add water to cover. Bring to a boil. Reduce heat; cook, uncovered, until almost tender, 6-8 minutes. Drain.
2. Meanwhile, in an ovenproof 12-in. skillet, cook and crumble sausage with onion over medium heat until no longer pink, 6-8 minutes. Remove from pan with a slotted spoon; wipe skillet clean.
3. In same pan, heat oil over medium-high heat. Add potatoes; sprinkle with salt and pepper. Cook until golden brown, 10-15 minutes, turning occasionally. Stir in sausage mixture. Remove from heat.
4. With the back of a spoon, make eight wells in potato mixture. Break one egg into each well. Sprinkle with cheese.
5. Bake until egg whites are set and yolks begin to thicken but are not hard, 12-15 minutes. Sprinkle with parsley.

1 serving: 460 cal., 29g fat (10g sat. fat), 234mg chol., 761mg sod., 29g carb. (4g sugars, 3g fiber), 21g pro.

Mixed Fruit with Lemon-Basil Dressing

TAKES: 15 min.
MAKES: 8 servings

2	Tbsp. lemon juice
½	tsp. sugar
¼	tsp. salt
¼	tsp. ground mustard
⅛	tsp. onion powder
	Dash pepper
6	Tbsp. olive oil
4½	tsp. minced fresh basil
1	cup cubed fresh pineapple
1	cup sliced fresh strawberries
1	cup sliced peeled kiwifruit
1	cup seedless watermelon balls
1	cup fresh blueberries
1	cup fresh raspberries

1. Place the lemon juice, sugar, salt, mustard, onion powder and pepper in a blender; cover and process for 5 seconds. While processing, gradually add oil in a steady stream. Stir in basil.

2. In a large bowl, combine the fruit. Drizzle with dressing and toss to coat. Refrigerate until serving.

¾ cup: 145 cal., 11g fat (1g sat. fat), 0 chol., 76mg sod., 14g carb. (9g sugars, 3g fiber), 1g pro.
Diabetic exchanges: 2 fat, 1 fruit.

Lemon-Lime Bars

PREP: 20 min. • **BAKE:** 20 min. + cooling • **MAKES:** 4 dozen

- 1 cup butter, softened
- ½ cup confectioners' sugar
- 2 tsp. grated lime zest
- 1¾ cups all-purpose flour
- ¼ tsp. salt

FILLING

- 4 large eggs, room temperature
- 1½ cups sugar
- ¼ cup all-purpose flour
- ½ tsp. baking powder
- ⅓ cup lemon juice
- 2 tsp. grated lemon zest
- Confectioners' sugar

1. Preheat oven to 350°. In a large bowl, cream butter and confectioners' sugar until light and fluffy. Beat in lime zest. Combine flour and salt; gradually add to creamed mixture and mix well.

2. Press into a greased 13x9-in. baking dish. Bake just until edges are lightly browned, 13-15 minutes.

3. Meanwhile, in another large bowl, beat eggs and sugar. Combine flour and baking powder. Gradually add to egg mixture. Stir in lemon juice and zest; beat until frothy. Pour over hot crust.

4. Bake until light golden brown, 20-25 minutes. Cool on a wire rack. Dust with confectioners' sugar. Cut into squares. Store in the refrigerator.

1 bar: 88 cal., 4g fat (2g sat. fat), 28mg chol., 60mg sod., 12g carb. (7g sugars, 0 fiber), 1g pro.

Tarragon Asparagus

TAKES: 15 min. • **MAKES:** 8 servings

- 2 lbs. fresh asparagus, trimmed
- 2 Tbsp. olive oil
- 1 tsp. salt
- ½ tsp. pepper
- ¼ cup honey
- 2 to 4 Tbsp. minced fresh tarragon

On a large plate, toss asparagus with oil, salt and pepper. Grill, covered, over medium heat until crisp-tender, 6-8 minutes, turning occasionally and basting frequently with honey during the last 3 minutes. Sprinkle with tarragon.

1 serving: 76 cal., 4g fat (1g sat. fat), 0 chol., 302mg sod., 11g carb. (10g sugars, 1g fiber), 2g pro.

Diabetic exchanges: 1 vegetable, ½ starch, ½ fat.

HANDCRAFTED WITH LOVE

Hand-Stamped Spring

Transform a basic kitchen towel into an Easter gift some-bunny is sure to love.

WHAT YOU'LL NEED
- Flour sack towel
- Peeps marshmallow bunnies
- Decoupage glue
- Fabric paint
- Hot glue gun
- Craft pompoms

DIRECTIONS
1. Wash and iron a plain white flour sack towel to create a smooth work surface.
2. Coat a few Peeps marshmallow bunnies with decoupage glue and dry thoroughly.
3. Dip one side of one marshmallow bunny into fabric paint and stamp on the towel to create your pattern of choice. Repeat with a fresh Peep and additional paint colors, if desired.
4. When the paint is dry, use a hot glue gun to attach craft pompoms for bunny tails.

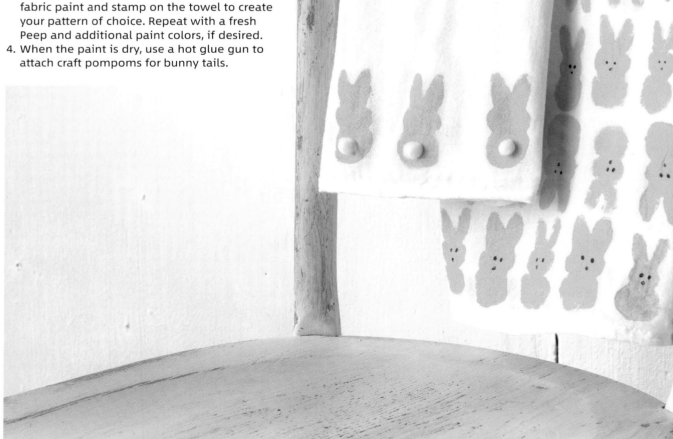

Tied Up in Knots

Old-fashioned macrame returns with a fresh twist for a hanging vase.

WHAT YOU'LL NEED
- 32 ft. of 2 mm jute twine
- Quart-size mason jar

DIRECTIONS
1. Cut twine into 8 equal pieces. Group in 2 bundles of 4 pieces.
2. Lay the 2 bundles of twine perpendicular to each other, crossing them in the middle. Tie them in a lanyard knot.
3. Separate 2 strands from 2 side-by-side bundles. Tie them in a knot 1½ in. above the lanyard knot. Repeat all the way around, until all the strands have been tied together.
4. Move another 1½ in. above the first row of knots and tie 2 more strands together, making sure to pull the strands from side-by-side knots and not the same section. This will create the diamond-shaped pattern. Repeat all the way around again.
5. Continue the pattern for 5 rows of knots. Gather the excess twine at the top and tie in a thick knot to use to hang the vase. Insert the mason jar, centering the bottom on the lanyard knot, and fill as desired.

Garden Variety

Adorn your door with springtime splendor.

WHAT YOU'LL NEED
- ½ yd. burlap fabric
- Embroidery floss
- Craft twigs
- Floral picks
- Greenery picks
- Pine cones
- Orange spray paint
- Decorative accents as desired
- Large-eye needle
- Hot glue gun

DIRECTIONS
1. Cut the burlap into 2 half-oval pieces 7¼ in. across. Use embroidery floss and needle to stitch pieces together along the bottom curve in a semicircle, keeping the top of the pouch open. Add ornamental stitches, if desired.
2. Wrap the craft twigs together and bend them to create a handle. Hot-glue the ends of the twigs to the top part of the bag.
3. Arrange the floral and greenery picks inside the bag, and adhere with hot glue.
4. Spray-paint the pine cones orange, and glue pieces of greenery to the flat end of each.
5. Glue pine cone carrots and any desired decorative accents to the outside.

Summer

Evening clouds roll over the
Tatoosh Range in Mount Rainier
National Park, Washington.
There, a lupine meadow blooms.
PHOTO BY MARY LIZ AUSTIN

THE GOOD LIFE

Goodbye City, Hello Country!

*Her family left California behind and hit the road
in search of a farm to call home.*

BY KELLEY BRACKEN *Rural Retreat, Virginia*

Excitement gripped us as the RV pulled out of our California driveway for the last time. I could hardly believe we were actually doing it.

Though my family lived in the city, we had always loved the idea of moving to the country. We were inspired by the stories and pictures in magazines like *Country*. As we learned more about where our food came from, our desire to live off the land grew stronger.

Then one day my parents, Philip and Lynda, always adventurous, decided to list our house for sale and see what would happen. Just like that, we sold our home, and in its place we bought a secondhand RV to live in.

My parents, sister Michelle and I left Los Angeles County, the only place I had ever called home, and drove to an unknown destination in search of a farm.

It was definitely an adventure. We drove to every corner of the country, visiting any farm that would let us learn and work there. After much searching, we put down roots in Rural Retreat, Virginia.

God blessed us more than we ever imagined, as the soft flowing streams, red barns and lush rolling pastures around us became home. We were welcomed by friendly neighbors who were excited about our farming vision.

To this day we are so grateful for the help and support of these neighbors who have become like family. We named our place My Shepherd's Farm, inspired by the words of Psalm 23, "The Lord is my shepherd; I shall not want."

Dad, born and raised in Ireland, was able to start reliving childhood memories. While picking cabbage to sell at our local farmer's market, he told Michelle and me

Country dad Philip loves living off the land. This life makes Kelley (right) and her sister, Michelle, jump for joy.

Pigs roam the pastures; Kelley's nieces explore after splashing in a nearby spring.

God blessed us more than we ever imagined, as the soft flowing streams, red barns and lush rolling pastures around us became home.

stories of how, as a boy, he would load his wheelbarrow full of homegrown cabbage to sell door to door in the early morning.

During the summers he spent at his uncle's farm, he imagined having a farm of his own one day. He has always been an extremely hard worker, and it is so wonderful to see him living his dream.

Today, most of what we eat we produce. We sell pastured pork, chicken and eggs along with our homemade deodorants, lip balms and soaps at the Wytheville and Abingdon farmers markets.

We also host a herdshare program that provides raw A2A2 milk to shareholders. We make our own hay, grow vegetable gardens, keep bees and do our own canning. We are learning how to raise our food sustainably, without hormones, antibiotics or pesticides.

Since moving to the farm, I've learned countless lessons, both directly and secondhand, through the experiences of those around me. I've done plenty of hard work and know that it is good. I know what it's like to have meals where everything on the plate was grown on our farmland, and I understand now that these flavors are unlike anything from the store.

I have learned that pigs are stronger than they look, and there is no need for a gym membership after hauling hay. I've tasted honey straight from the hive and watched as hens hatch and raise their chicks with such care.

It's true that you never really get to the bottom of a to-do list on a farm. But I've come to appreciate the blooms of spring so much more after spending winter breaking ice.

I've learned how much electric fence can hurt. I've experienced sleeping in a field with a cow about to calve and raising friendly cows that respond to their names.

A normally tame sow showed me she can run quite fast after she's had piglets; in the process, Michelle showed me how fast she can hop a fence. I've watched kids from the city delight in the joys of farm life for the first time.

We've spent whole evenings catching lightning bugs in mason jars, swinging on the porch swing and gazing at the stars. We have ridden cows and pigs, and we've face-planted in the mud when the overzealous pigs have run to greet us at once.

Some days on the farm are long and hard, and they don't look or feel like anything that belongs in a magazine. On these days we step back and remind ourselves that we are living the dream.

My family has created so many memories for which we are grateful to God, and we are excited to know we have so much yet to learn. ☀

Lessons in a Growing Field

*A slow harvest fails to dim this young
Minnesotan's passion for organic farming.*

BY ANDREW BARSNESS *Hoffman, Minnesota*

I'm Andrew Barsness, an organic grain farmer in Minnesota. My grandparents were farmers; I was a college freshman when they passed away in 2010. With the future of the family farm in question, I decided to try my hand at farming. Lacking an ag background, I learned how to farm through a mishmash of resources: online farm forums, equipment manuals, my grandfather's notes, YouTube, neighborly advice, my mom, lots of trial and error—and, eventually, a degree in agricultural systems management with a focus in farm and ranch management from the University of Minnesota.

I farm 156 of the farm's 270 tillable acres, renting the land from my mom and aunt. I started transitioning this part of the farm to organic in 2016; it became officially certified in 2018. I'm growing soybeans only, although I've grown other grains, including corn and wheat.

I've found farming to be a lifestyle and an occupation that fits me like a glove. I cherish the freedom and independence it provides and the creativity and entrepreneurship it demands. And I often think of my grandfather. Reminders of him are all over the farm, from parts he hung on shed walls to tools and equipment I use on a daily basis. This makes me feel connected to him as a grandson and as a fellow farmer. I am proud to be following in his footsteps.

I've outlined here a typical week as a farmer.

MONDAY I spent most of the day scouting my soybean fields. The plants have established a pretty good canopy to help shade out new weed growth, and the pods are getting bigger and starting to fill with beans.

Earlier in the year I experienced a substantial infestation of soybean aphids. Fortunately recent heavy rains seem to have reduced aphid numbers to the point where they're no longer a major concern. There aren't many cost-effective options for dealing with pests or diseases in an organic system, so crop rotation and variety selection are extremely important.

TUESDAY Today I cultivated 60 acres of soybeans. Of my three fields, this is definitely the best. In my opinion, weed control is the biggest challenge of growing organic grain crops. I'm proud to have produced a relatively weed-free field of soybeans without using any herbicides. I refer to that field as my "proof of concept field," in response to the doubters and critics who don't believe organic farming is a viable method of grain production. It also helps quell some of the self-doubt that inevitably creeps in from time to time.

My loan officer from the USDA Farm Service Agency came out to see how things were going. We looked at all my equipment and crops. While walking through the proof of concept field, he mentioned that my crop looks "better than a lot of the conventional (nonorganic) fields" he's seen. It was a definite morale booster.

WEDNESDAY I finished getting the old John Deere 6620 combine prepped and ready for harvest. I also changed and checked the fluids and filters on the combine, made sure the settings were right for harvesting soybeans, and blew off any grain dust or chaff that I missed last fall. Keeping the combine maintained and clean is essential for preventing fires, which are surprisingly common during harvest. Soybean dust is notoriously prone to catching fire. The dry, incredibly fine dust accumulates on the combine and can ignite as a result of heat from the engine and exhaust, bad bearings, or the sparks from static or exposed wires.

Andrew stepped in to take over his grandparents' farm, learning on the fly.

From top, Andrew Barsness (with his father, Dave) positions an auger for transferring grain into a bin; prepares to move soybeans along in the grain truck; and harvests soybeans with a combine.

During my first year of farming, my combine was destroyed by fire. When I woke up the next morning, my neighbors were out in the field harvesting the remainder of my crop—an act of kindness I'll never forget. My grandfather had a combine fire not too many years prior, so we have two generations of burned combines.

THURSDAY Today I spent time planning for the future. Within the next several years I'll likely need to invest in some newer equipment and additional grain storage. Adequate grain storage is particularly important for organic farmers. Conventional farmers usually have a grain buyer close enough to allow convenient shipping from the field directly to the buyer at any time. They can harvest the grain, load it onto a truck and drive it to town on the same day. But organic grain buyers are few and far between. As a result, organic farmers often have to sell grain to a buyer much farther away or in an entirely different state, which often necessitates storing it all on the farm in the meantime.

FRIDAY After scouting the fields again, I determined that 60 acres are looking great, 40 acres are in good condition, 30 acres are decent and another 30 are very poor. We had a bad drought in early spring followed by rain that didn't stop for a month. A few days ago there was a hazardous weather warning in effect predicting large hail, 75 mph winds, tornadoes and flash flooding. If any of that had actually materialized, my crops would have been done for. Right now I'm hoping for warmer weather so my soybeans can reach full maturity before we get a hard frost. As a farmer, I've learned to accept that there's a lot out of my control. Even if you do everything right, things will inevitably go wrong. You just have to plan and prepare for every possible outcome and hope for the best.

EPILOGUE On Oct. 10, we did get a hard frost, which damaged roughly two-thirds of the crop. Subsequent rain and snow made the bean pods damp and tough to thresh with a combine harvester. Frost-damaged soybeans further complicated the process. I finally finished harvesting soybeans in early December. The yields ended up being quite poor because of the weather. However, I've gained some confidence in knowing I can succeed at organic weed control when the weather is at least somewhat cooperative.

With all the inherent hardships in farming, people might wonder why anyone would ever want to be a farmer. I farm because it's the only path I've ever truly been passionate about. I appreciate getting dirty, and I like being outside in the fresh air, working with my hands and seeing my crops grow. I'm grateful for the opportunity to preserve and improve the land I'm responsible for, and I hope to build something I can pass along to any children I may have someday. ☀

Cherish Every Moment

Each day brings new gifts from the countryside that surrounds this home.

BY SHIRLEY STUBY *Schellsburg, Pennsylvania*

Living along a country road amid the foothills of the Allegheny Mountains is country living at its best. Through the large expanse of our living room windows, I can watch the farms and wildlife that surround our home.

There's less hassle and traffic out here than living in a city. We listen to the neighbor's rooster crow in the morning and watch herds of deer in our front yard. Lyle, my husband, also puts up many birdhouses and feeders.

In the springtime, I hear the *putt-putt* of a farmer's John Deere or the quiet whir of a Cub Cadet plowing the small gardens in the neighborhood.

Peaches, cherries and apples grow on the ridge nearby. Birds tweet while looking for worms, and bees buzz as they pollinate the fruit blossoms.

During the summer, corn and soybean planters, hay balers and rakes go from field to field, traveling up and down the hill beside us. Loads and more loads of hay go from the fields to the barns, to be stored for winter.

Calves are born in the field across the road, and mother cows cry out to babies that explore too far.

In fall, changing leaves paint a colorful picture on the mountain beyond the road. Huge combines fill the valley, slowly chugging their way to fields planted with grains, now ready for harvest. Soybean pickers fill the waiting trucks, and farmers are anxious to sell their crop at a good price. Wild turkeys amble along as they glean from the newly cleared fields.

Rows of apple trees line the hills and ridges, standing like soldiers. Branches almost touch the ground with their heavy load of fruit, ripe and ready for picking.

Winter is a time to sit back and relax. I am secure in my cozy home while watching the snow fall. The snow brings thoughts of plowing our driveway, making snow angels, and picking our Christmas tree. It also prompts the making of lists—cookies to bake, groceries for the holiday meals, and gifts for family and friends.

My husband and I both grew up on farms in central and western Pennsylvania. I was a banker for all of my career, but am now retired. With more free time, Lyle and I love making memories with our grandchildren.

For a few years we raised miniature donkeys but sold them so we would have more opportunities to travel. We have visited all 50 states and are now starting over. We drive the back roads so we can get a look at country living in every corner of America.

The seasons, roaming animals and harvesttime make life in the country special. The peace and serenity I feel cannot be touched as I count stars, glimpse the man in the moon or watch a blaze of orange fill the sky with a beautiful sunrise. But most of all, I love hearing thunder and seeing lightning flash during a summer storm. ☀

Lyle shows the corn was way above knee-high on the Fourth of July.

Clockwise from top: Roses surround the deck; cattle graze across the road; a double rainbow arches over farmland; the flag painted by Lyle and his brother, Gordon, graces the barn on the family farm; making hay in the front yard.

Home Is Where the Herd Is

A sanctuary for surrendered animals brings families to the farm.

BY JASON MULLINS *Trumann, Arkansas*

I was recently approached by a woman at a local gardening seminar where I was the guest speaker. "You don't look like a farmer," she said to me. Considering the many hats I wear, I can see why she would feel that way. I have a minister's license, a bachelor's degree in radiologic sciences and a fast-paced career in medical imaging. Of course, in complete contrast to all of that, I also run Fair Haven Farms, a small farm in northeast Arkansas.

Much like Old MacDonald, we've got nearly every animal you can think of on our farm—more than 400 total from about 24 species. This sanctuary, staffed primarily by my wife, Tabithia, and me, is a permanent home for rescued or owner-surrendered animals.

During the process of building our farm, or perhaps during the process of the farm building us, we serendipitously launched an agritourism venture that continues to grow each season. You might say we have a very unconventional approach to farm living.

A Craigslist ad put us on the road to Lakeland, Tennessee, in the spring of 2010, for what would be the beginning of our adventure in agritourism. In Lakeland, we found the cutest chocolate miniature donkey foal we had ever laid eyes on. Festus, as he would soon be called, made the hourlong journey home with us safely secured in the bed of our truck. We didn't even own a trailer at that time.

We were so happy with how Festus settled into our farm that soon we found a second ad beckoning to be answered. Shortly thereafter, there was another ad, and another and another—and the rest is history.

We started bringing in llamas, donkeys, horses, goats, ducks, chickens, rabbits and pigs in high volume. Before long, locals started to notice our little zoo on Ozark Avenue. We invited a nearby school to come visit and began hosting community events, including the Trumann Wild Duck Festival.

Just as the number of our animals has climbed a little at a time, so has the number of programs and services we offer to the public. We host birthday celebrations year-round. Even with snow on the ground, we load the trailer with a variety of animals to deliver what we like to call "agri-tainment" to eagerly waiting guests.

We travel around the area to provide our petting zoo to schools, nursing facilities, fundraisers, baby showers, festivals and just about any other event you can imagine. On every trip we make, we realize the importance of the work we are committed to.

Children enjoy hitching a ride on a wagon during a farm camp at Fair Haven Farms.

Unbelievably, many people, adults and children alike, rarely have the opportunity to encounter animals aside from domestic dogs and cats. Their reactions to Oli the "llampaca" (our llama/alpaca crossbreed) and the rest of the crew are often worth more than any fees we receive.

We have helped individuals overcome their fears, been an outlet for the grief-stricken and listened to

Farm visitors get to interact with animals such as chickens, Oli the llampaca and a pretty, posing pig.

Moments like these make the sometimes difficult and hectic journey worth every mile we've traveled.

seniors recollect a lifetime of memories. Moments like these make the sometimes difficult and hectic journey worth every mile we've traveled.

After years of working at various festivals hosted by other groups, we decided we should host an event of our own. With that thought, Barn Boo was born. Costumed animals, games, concessions and vendors make this fall event a huge hit.

Summer programs offered us another opportunity for growth. We are now in our sixth year of hosting farm camps. These two-day camps bring kids to the farm for hands-on learning, which is good for the soul and the animals alike. The camps are so popular that we've had to add sessions in each of the past three years. Some of our campers love it so much they return every week. The regulars are like members of the family.

In May 2016, we hosted our first Spring Barnival, and that festival brought in even more revenue than the Barn Boo. And we had another great turnout for the 2017 Spring Barnival. Heavy rains the night before meant Saturday morning was a race to finish setting up. Most agritourism depends on weather, and we've had our share of dealing with adverse conditions.

We provide free booth space at our events to help out local producers and crafters, many of whom are just starting out. They learn what works and get to observe others who may have been at this longer.

Once Spring Barnival and farm camps are over for the year, the Arkansas summer heats up and no one really wants to be out on a farm. Just to stay relevant, we hold a few Dollar Days to give families a fun outing and provide an open house to showcase our farm services.

When we add a Christmas event, which is still a work in progress, we will offer events in all four seasons.

It seems that, even in our rural area, fewer people have access to the old farms we visited as kids.

Our farm has been a great way for us to make our living. We have worked hard for several years to build a customer base as well as status in our community. Working with local media outlets and through social media to create word-of-mouth buzz keeps us plenty busy. We haven't spent any money on advertising during our seven years. Now that we have regulars who come back for visits and events, we're just as happy to see them as they are to see Oli.

I may not look like a farmer, but after all these years I can barely go anywhere in our community without hearing little voices calling out, "There's Farmer Jason!" ☀

Like Father, Like Daughter

Dad sacrificed a lot to keep the family in the country, and it's a life they treasure.

BY LEAH LEACH *Waynesboro, Tennessee*

My childhood was ideal, running free, wading in mud puddles and hunting for bird nests. I heard great horned owls at night and ate juicy, sun-warmed tomatoes off the vine. I took it all for granted, like the air I breathed and the delicious water that came from our well.

Back when my daddy was 12 years old, his family moved from their farm to a house in town. He spent the next 30 years working to return to the rural lifestyle he had loved as a boy. After I was born, he and Mama bought 5 acres on which they kept horses and raised chickens, goats and a milk cow. Mama canned fruits and vegetables from our garden. We raised our own meat.

Daddy still worked a corporate job, rising at 4:30 a.m. to milk our cow, and then commuting an hour in order to afford a home in the country. Catching a whiff of Bag Balm on his hands kept him sane in business meetings.

My siblings and I would run down our dirt road to wait for Daddy's car at the end of the day. We stuck out our thumbs like hitchhikers, and Daddy would give us a ride home. The car smelled like new upholstery, and Daddy wore a tie. But once home, he changed into jeans, boots and a faded Wrangler shirt. Together, we would feed the animals. Then we would eat a meal that we had grown ourselves.

As I grew older, I wanted to see new places and experience new things. But after the birth of my first child, I realized I wanted my children to have the same childhood I had enjoyed.

Now, my children feel grass under their bare feet and catch fireflies on summer evenings. They know the calls of whippoorwills; they eat carrots from the garden; they splash in mud puddles; and they feel the wonder of a new baby calf in the pasture. When my sons work alongside their daddy, when my little girls beg to check cows with him, when I pull the first radish from the garden, I am overwhelmed with gratitude for my daddy's years of sacrifice. I will never take this life for granted. ☀

Sisters Leah and Stephanie loved the country. Dad Del (on Sir with Leah), endured an hour-long commute to give his children a rural childhood.

Family Pig Party

When you can't leave the farm, the vacation comes home.

BY BETH M. HOWARD *Donnellson, Iowa*

It started 40 years ago, when two brothers, Dennis and Doug Seyb, invited a few friends over to their 1,000-acre farm in southeastern Iowa for a Labor Day weekend fish fry. Dennis loved to fish and was looking for a way to share his catch of bluegill from the farm's ponds. The brothers bought a few cases of beer and set up some lawn chairs—and a tradition was born.

The following year they invited a few more friends, who brought friends themselves, and the Seyb brothers started thinking: With this growing crowd, why not roast a pig? After all, they had hogs on their farm. From that point on, the Seyb Family Annual Pig Party became official. They even have T-shirts made, and each year they feature a new pig-themed design. A local ambulance driver who moonlights as an artist has helped with the design for years.

Because livestock farmers can never leave their animals—which means forgoing vacations—Dennis and Doug decided to turn the pig roast into a short "staycation"

With great anticipation, Doug and Dennis Seyb check on the progress of the pig.

for themselves and expanded the weekend's festivities, along with the guest list. Friends and relatives from Oklahoma, Wisconsin, Chicago, Pennsylvania, Canada and even Switzerland come to spend time with the Seyb brothers. I've had fun being a part of it for five years.

The pig party now starts Friday night with a supper of pork loin sandwiches for the early arrivals. (Guests park RVs next to Doug's barn or sleep in "the bunkhouse," the old family home next door.) Saturday includes a daylong float trip down the Des Moines River, with 20 kayaks, canoes and inner tubes all roped together in one big moving picnic, as the current carries everyone and their snacks downstream. Saturday night, the group gathers at the home of Dennis and his wife, Liza Alton, for a fish fry, a nod to the pig roast's origin.

On Sunday, Doug gets up before dawn to fire up the roaster, and I hold a pie class starting at around 10 a.m. to guide a dozen or more party guests through the baking process, resulting in a smorgasbord of pies to

Family and friends relax at sunset. The canoes in the back are still drying out from the previous day's float trip.

serve at the evening's big event. Liza has her hands in many of the weekend's details—she rounds up the pig-themed decorations, helps make pies and spearheads the creation of new T-shirts.

The crowd starts to gather by 3 p.m. Guests bring their own lawn chairs, coolers and a dish to share. The granary, which Doug power-washes and lines with temporary food shelves, is filled with slow cookers and cheesy casseroles, appetizers, salads, homemade bread, barbecue sauce, brownies and "berry-licious," a farm-famous dessert made of whipped cream and berries. A buffet the length of a semi gets overcrowded, but enough space is always reserved for the heaping trays of roast pork.

When the pig is off the roaster it's heaved onto a huge slab of plywood supported by sawhorses. A team of volunteers in aprons and rubber gloves carves while both guests and dogs hover about, hoping to get scraps.

Partygoers, dressed in shorts or overalls, stream in faster and faster, and the gravel road is lined with cars on both sides. They know the food is served at 6 p.m. and the band plays at 7. Folk musicians strum their banjos and play their fiddles on the porch while families dine around picnic tables and kids run around waving sparklers or playing tag, cornhole or volleyball. The whole scene looks like a miniature county fair.

The party used to stretch well past midnight and the beer kegs would run dry, but that's changed a bit, too. Most local guests leave by 10 p.m. these days. But don't let the early night fool you: There will be no stopping the staycation tradition. The Seybs—along with their children and a growing number of grandchildren—plan to keep it going for at least another 40 years. That's going to be a lot of T-shirts. ☀

Clockwise from top left: Friends carve up the roasted pig while a hungry pooch waits for scraps; Liza Alton and her sister Amy Alton-Stonebrook strike a pose during the annual Des Moines River float trip; just like an annual race or concert tour, new T-shirt designs are created every year for the Labor Day weekend party; guests line up outside the granary to serve themselves dinner; Dennis and Liza's great-nephews Sam and George momentarily pause from eating.

SCRAPBOOK

**My daughter's curls were wild with the humidity, and the watermelon juice
running down her chin make this the perfect summertime picture.**
JASON GIRVEN *Sugar Run, Pennsylvania*

Our grandchildren pick black heart cherries, chase lightning bugs and help my husband, Wes, and me plant seeds in the garden on our farm. Here Aniston leads her baby brother Ronin to the barn for some summer fun.
LYNN CARR *Cool Ridge, West Virginia*

This Oklahoma farm captivated my heart from the first time I remember grabbing a camera and strolling the fields. I realized, without doubt, this is the life I want, always.
SUNNY HERRMANN *Agra, Oklahoma*

My son Harley loves this old Ford pedal tractor, which belonged to his dad when he was a boy.
Here, Harley is "working" the field, pulling a wagon filled with his friends, his blanket and his football.
AMBER HERSH *Carr, Colorado*

A beautiful Anna's hummingbird appeared as I was
taking photos near the Bay Bridge in San Francisco.
RACHEL VANDEMARK *Longwood, Florida*

My daughter Adeline and this goat have the same
expression, and her pigtails and the goat's ears match.
JESSICA ROBERTS *Camarillo, California*

Derby, a miniature donkey, lets Maxine hitch a ride on his back.
RICHARD FISCHER *Calico Rock, Arkansas*

My dear friend shows how ranchers used to grease windmills—climbing up to the platform to do it by hand.
BETH GIBBONS *Crawford, Nebraska*

Samuel, the biggest little cowboy we know, gives his mare lots of "scratchies."
HANNAH STROM *Lake Park, Minnesota*

It's hard to tell who is more excited to help feed the calves—my dog
Rita or my grandson Evan.
NANCY VANDRIE *Marion, Michigan*

I marveled at this stunning sky on my nightly walk. The moment was so beautiful, it almost brought tears to my eyes.

MELISSA HALL *Kingman, Arizona*

Peaches, Stripe and Strawberry range freely around our farm.
They love to hang out on an old rocking chair on the cabin porch.
LAUREN McCAMMON *Prince Frederick, Maryland*

Competing on my horse Frosty, Kenly Kelso, my 8-year-old great-granddaughter, won a junior princess title. I raised this horse myself, and I still ride at age 86. We are the best team, my great-granddaughter, Frosty and me.
CHARLES McKAY *Mount Pleasant, Utah*

At Medora's hot air balloon festival, wind kept the balloonists close to the ground.
KATHERINE PLESSNER *Verona, North Dakota*

My grandmother gave me a start of gooseneck loosestrife years ago, and the butterflies absolutely adore it.
AMY TIPTON *Erwin, Tennessee*

My granddaughter Paisley peeks out of the barn, dreaming of adventure.
JACQUIE PARR *Santa Rosa, California*

We paddled across the lake to this tiny island under the Milky Way on a summer night. Nothing says country life like stargazing.
HEIDI NOVAK *Pine City, Minnesota*

Our grandson Carson savored the harvest of our wild cherries!
KATHIE KUMMET *Culdesac, Idaho*

Years ago, I learned my husband, Dave, preferred time at home more than vacations to faraway places. Thus began the transformation of our gardens into a country getaway.
JERELYN McKINLEY *Dola, Ohio*

The garden means so much to my family, and we all cherish it, each in our own way.
This oasis touches the hearts of all who enter.
JOLIE RAIMONDO *Waverly, Minnesota*

After showing her cow, Becky and her friend Daffodil slept quietly in the straw.
SANDY KLINE *New Haven, Connecticut*

While at my aunt and uncle's farm in Powhatan, Virginia,
I watched these male and female eastern tiger swallowtails.
PARKS ROUNTREY *Mechanicsville, Virginia*

My cousin Kirklyn broke out the bubbles when rain
interrupted a baseball game at our great-granny's house.
REBECCA FINCHUM *Strawberry Plains, Tennessee*

Baylor, my 2-year-old son, is the sixth generation on our ranch.
SHELBY HILL *Tonto Basin, Arizona*

This common yellowthroat looked anything but common as it sang in a field of purple lupines in Rangeley, Maine.
CHRISTOPHER CICCONE *Woburn, Massachusetts*

This runt piglet and adorable puppy became fast friends.
CATHY COOPER *Covington, Indiana*

Gathering eggs is my daughter's favorite chore on the farm.
Cora is compassionate and has a strong sense of responsibility.
SARA ROGERS *Coxs Creek, Kentucky*

FEEL THE LOVE OF COUNTRY

HEART & SOUL

White Lammas wheat grows on the Palouse Colony Farm's rolling hills.

ROLLING HILLS: CHRISTINE HAINES; PALOUSE RIVER: DON SCHEUERMAN

Golden Waves of Grain

A Washington family grows heritage crops in a spectacular setting.

BY RICHARD D. SCHEUERMAN *Richland, Washington*

Every single day during my primary school years in Endicott, Washington, my school bus passed by the Palouse Colony Farm's beautiful undulating hills. I was just fascinated by the place. The farm sits along the Palouse River at the end of a steep gravel road that runs down a pine-covered rocky bluff. The grassy slopes of the bluff abound with deer, pheasants and waterfowl.

My family descends from the first settlers in the area, German farmers from Russia's Volga region who had immigrated to America's Pacific Northwest in 1889, setting up the Palouse Colony in the sheltered canyon of the Palouse River. From seeds they'd brought, they raised golden fields of wheat and barley.

I grew up in the 1960s, and I can recall my grandpa Karl Scheuerman and other family elders telling tales about mysterious happenings and the harsh living conditions endured during the early days of the colony. The northern lights scared the first settlers, as the multi-colored sky seemed to announce the end of the world.

The Palouse River's sheltered canyon has been home to the Ochs and Scheuerman families since the late 1800s.

The Palouse Colony Farm is special to our family, and Don, Rod and I are honored to be stewards of this magical place.

And once, fearing a whiteout blizzard, the teacher at the colony's two-room schoolhouse sent all the children home early, tying them together to save them from straying off the road toward the precipitous bluff overlooking the farm. I moved to Seattle once I reached adulthood, but I often thought fondly of that old family lore and my happy childhood memories of the area.

During my many fall hunting trips to the Palouse, an idea took shape: What if I could grow the same grains that had fed my ancestors? I visited the Fort Nisqually Living History Museum near Tacoma. While there, I learned that significant amounts of what was recorded as white, red and yellow wheat and some barley were raised during the 1820s and 1830s in the Pacific Northwest. Through additional

research—including a journey to the National Agricultural Library in Maryland—I identified the early grains my ancestors had grown: White Lammas and Sonoran Gold wheat. In 2014, my brother, Don, our cousin Rod Ochs and I started Palouse Heritage, a small heritage grain business. Our good friends lent us farmland where we grew Sonoran Gold wheat and Scots Bere barley, two of North America's oldest cereal grains.

A portion of the original Palouse Colony Farm was put up for sale in 2015. Since the 1990s, the land had been owned by a goat farmer who had the ground in pasture. Don, Rod and I pooled our resources to buy 20 acres of fertile river bottomland, the original barn and a house where the German immigrants lived while adjusting to life in America. Our land includes 5 acres of the rugged bluff overlooking the farm that supports native bunchgrass, glorious wild sunflowers and other shrub-steppe species. It's been my lifelong dream to own this property.

We rolled up our sleeves in spring 2015, removing weed-infested fence lines and fixing some of the original outbuildings. Thanks to the help of neighbors and longtime friends in area farm-supply businesses, we have assembled a rainbow coalition of used farm equipment including a red tractor, box drills, faded green weeders, a cultivator, and a rusted disk that may have predated the advent of paint.

A southward view of the Palouse dappled by rays of sunlight.

That first summer we raised a bumper crop of Sonoran Gold. This type of soft white wheat is thought by agricultural historians to be the first cereal grain grown here in the American West. We have yet to buy a combine, given the expense, so we rely on a kind neighbor for custom harvesting. For the second year of production, we also obtained seed for heritage malting barleys and for White Lammas wheat. We teamed up with Washington State University agronomists Stephen Jones and Steve Lyon for some considerable detective work, and we learned that a conscientious USDA plant explorer had introduced White Lammas to the Pacific Northwest in 1916 when he took a sample of the grain with him to the area.

Today, we grow 11 varieties of landrace, or ancient, grains that we sell in the form of artisan baking flours at *palouseheritage .com* and to local bakeries. We also turn our grains into culinary malts used for craft beer brewing.

One meaningful aspect of our work has been rediscovering how our ancestors lived when they first came to America. In addition to growing grain, they established a shared commons for grazing and substantial gardens. They tended long, narrow fields to conserve soil in three-crop rotations of fall wheat, spring barley or oats, and rye. Their Turkey Red, the first hard red bread wheat in the American West, revolutionized U.S. culinary history.

We revived this beautiful grain at Palouse Colony Farm in 2016. Some of our immigrant forebears first lived in simple homes dug into the sides of nearby slopes to provide winter shelter. Many of these were later converted to immense two-room concrete cellars to safeguard a cornucopia of canned produce and crocks holding sauerkraut, pickles and tiny watermelons. Two of these cellars are still visible on the land. Our forebears raised potatoes and cabbages, tended dairy and beef cattle and draft horses, and planted an orchard that still yields apples. They grew sunflowers, using the seeds to make cooking oil. They used the sunflower stalks to create a kind of syrup. Every spring, bushy heirloom hop vines burst forth in clusters along the base of the river bluff. The summer buds provided yeast for sourdough breads.

These days, the entire family often gathers at the farm: my wife, Lois, and I; daughter Mary, her husband, Charles, and their sons, 7-year-old Zachary and 6-year-old Micah; son Karl, his wife, Sara, along with their daughters, 5-year-old Annalise, 3-year-old Emily and 1-year-old Macey; and daughter Leigh. Don lives on the property, and we pile into the three bedrooms in his old house when we spend the night. Zachary and Micah help me collect apples from Don's garden to stock our fruit stand. They also gather potatoes, carrots and beets that we use to make borscht.

Our 93-year-old mother, Mary, lives close by in Endicott with my sister, Debbie. Andrew, Debbie's son, also lives in Endicott, and he helps us with the farming. Don's daughter, Nicole, often stays at the farm, too. When the family is together, we make sauerkraut from cabbage that we raise in the garden. The Palouse Colony Farm is special to everyone in our family, and Don, Rod and I are very honored to be stewards of this magical place. ☀

Richard Scheuerman, son-in-law Charles Rhoden and grandsons Micah and Zachary harvest White Lammas wheat; Crimson Turkey wheat makes ideal sourdough bread.

Love at First Bray

This rescued donkey was afraid of strangers—until he met a young boy.

BY JUDY MOORE *Florence, Montana*

My ranch in the Bitterroot Valley is home to an assortment of farm animals. At present, there are three horses, two dogs and two donkeys.

In 2009, I rescued one of those donkeys, Bo. Despite a successful rehab, he remained skittish around strangers unless I escorted them. But the walls came down when Bo met my grandson, Dylan.

Just shy of 4 years old, Dylan came with his mom and dad, Stacy and Aaron, to spend the Fourth of July with me in 2015. They were on their way to Canada for a vacation.

While keeping his distance from other family members, Bo displayed an unusual fascination with Dylan. Perhaps he had never seen such a tiny person close-up. We decided to introduce them.

As Dylan's parents stood nearby, I led the way, telling Dylan, "Move slowly, keep your arms down, be quiet and stoop down sometimes." He cautiously approached Bo, holding a rubber currycomb.

Step by step Dylan moved closer, and Bo held his ground. He seemed intrigued by this little visitor. Dylan softly rubbed Bo's shoulders and neck, removing some remnants of a thick winter coat.

It's hard for a 4-year-old to stay still for long, and impulse overcame restraint. Dylan made one quick move, sending Bo scampering off.

Not an auspicious start, but Bo and Dylan were not ready to give up. To witness a preschooler learn to control himself in such a short time was amazing. He approached Bo again and began currying.

Dylan's parents and I watched as true love developed between this once-untrustful donkey and a gentle boy. There was no fear or thought that Bo would be hurt in any way.

Over the next few days, Bo let Dylan throw his arms around his neck, pet his legs, hold his head in

Bo's skittish nature vanished when he bonded with his young friend, Dylan.

his hands and even pat his cheeks. And Dylan felt free to sit at Bo's feet while Bo carefully nibbled his shirt collar and hair and rubbed Dylan's back with his bristly chin.

Just as Dylan was calm, earning Bo's trust, Bo showed incredible restraint in all his movements with Dylan. He hugged Dylan (yes, a donkey can hug) without knocking him off balance.

They met again one week later as the family passed through on their return trip. It was almost dark, but Dylan and his dad trekked to the far reaches of the pasture. Bo came enthusiastically to meet them.

Since this encounter, Bo has been a changed donkey, trusting people unless they make quick moves. Bo's farrier says she can't believe it and that Dylan is a miracle worker. ☀

Giving from the Family Garden

Her grandparents' love and generosity helped feed and rebuild their community.

BY KARIE CHATHAM *Mount Olive, Mississippi*

Growing up, I'd never heard the term "community garden." I suppose it's more common in larger cities, where a garden at home is not always possible, but the benefits of a community garden are vast—and in a way, thanks to my grandparents, I've had one all my life.

My brother and I grew up picking corn and peas in the early summer mornings on my grandparents' farm, when school was out and our parents worked during the day. We would pick, complain and pile our produce in 5-gallon buckets at the end of the rows.

Neighbors would drive up and talk to Grandpa from their cars, and he always offered them corn or peas or whatever else we were picking. I couldn't believe it—we had worked so hard on it! But as I grew older, I realized that giving food was better than a store-bought gift. Food takes time, money and patience. It's a gift with love behind it.

My grandparents are the most giving people I know. I started sixth grade just before Hurricane Katrina hit in 2005. My family, extended and immediate, all waited

Grandpa taught Karie the joy of sharing homegrown food with the community.

out the storm together. Power was out and businesses closed for a while, so I spent time off school with my family. My grandfather donated supplies to people in town from the back of a truck, and my brother and I helped Grandpa hand them out.

During the rebuilding, my grandmother once cooked all of our frozen vegetables and meat, loaded it all up in the back of her vehicle, and drove to where utility workers were repairing power lines. People had come from all over the country to help out, and she was determined to feed at least some of them. Once again, my brother and I helped. We drove up, popped open the trunk and got to work. That day, we served complete strangers home-cooked meals from the pots and pans in Grandma's car.

A garden is wonderful, but a community is what makes the scorching sun, the sweat and the bending over worthwhile. I hope people in cities are able to grow their own food, whether in backyards or a community garden alongside neighbors, because connection and food-sharing are what make having a garden special. I'm lucky to have had something like it my entire life. ☀

Elizabeth Has a Little Lamb

My daughter's first 4-H project taught her to rise above heartbreak.

BY MOLLY BALINT *Churchville, Maryland*

There's a part of the county fair that I skim over every year. It's one of the hardest parts for our girls—Mary, Emma, Elizabeth—and for me. But at the same time, it's one of the most important pieces of the girls' 4-H experience. The reality is that the lambs we buy in the spring for the project are raised for their meat and sold in an auction at the end of the fair.

For 4-H kids, this comes with lots of responsibility. If there ever was an opportunity to understand and honor where your food comes from, there's not much that matches raising it yourself. Not only are they learning about the sources of their food, they are part of the process.

The lambs are treated with respect, kindness and gentleness. They are nurtured and loved, and for the time that they are in our care, given the best home possible.

But despite the fact that we all know how this story is going to end, hearts still manage to become entwined with these four-legged woolly animals.

For my girls, the goodbyes come on Saturday night. The excitement of the auction in the show ring barn is mingled with dread of what's to come. It's not easy for them, but they understand.

The 2016 fair was different. For starters, it was Elizabeth's first year showing, and she is my tender-hearted child. When she was younger, she got especially attached to one of Emma's lambs and sobbed the whole way home from the fair.

To complicate things even more, Elizabeth and her lamb, Nora, became attached to each other.

During the first few days of the fair, people stood outside our pen, looking Nora over. Many thought we had one of the best-looking lambs there. And while this may seem like an exciting prospect, it left us quite torn. If Nora won the show, we would have to sell her. The grand and reserve grand champion lambs must go through the auction.

So I asked Elizabeth if she would like to pull Nora from the show. After much discussion, Elizabeth said she wanted to go for it. She was going to put Nora in the show.

And then the bittersweet happened: Nora won reserve grand champion. We were thrilled, but I have to admit my heart sank a bit when the judge shook her hand and gave her the big purple ribbon.

When auction night arrived, Elizabeth seemed OK. I thought about trying to buy Nora back, but I knew I might not be able to afford it. And I hated to give Elizabeth any false hope.

As Elizabeth and I stood together waiting for her turn to go into the sale ring, suddenly she looked at me as her face twisted up and she started to cry. I wiped her tears and whispered in her ear how proud I was of her.

...hearts still manage to become entwined with these four-legged woolly animals.

When her turn came to walk in the ring, Elizabeth managed to pull herself together. But her red, puffy eyes gave away her sadness.

I stood in the back and listened as the price climbed higher and higher. When the gavel dropped and Nora was sold, I was discouraged to find out she'd been bought by a bank. I figured a bank would be unwilling to lose money and let me buy Nora.

Elizabeth and I pushed through the crowds to find Nora's buyer standing in the back. His name was John Eaton and he worked for PeoplesBank. We thanked him for his support of 4-H kids. Then I explained the situation to him and asked if there would be any way he'd consider letting us buy Nora.

Before the words were all out of my mouth, John stopped me. He told us that he had a flock of sheep on his farm. He said that Nora was a nice lamb and he told us to keep her. Not every fair ends this way, but it worked out.

I'm proud of the hard work my girls are doing. And I'm truly thankful for people who give so freely, like that kind banker in the back corner of the sale barn. ☀

John, Nora's buyer, was moved by Elizabeth's love for her ewe lamb. Elizabeth, who raised Nora as a 4-H project, had mixed feelings on winning reserve grand champion.

Never Too Old for Home

Every time we cast a line, Daddy and I catch memories that are bigger than any fish in the lake.

BY AMIE ROLLAND *Shreveport, Louisiana*

A dad is every child's hero—if they're lucky, as I am, to have a great one. I'm an English teacher in Beijing, China, who was born and raised in north Louisiana. After I moved away, my folks sold our home and bought a new place on the lake.

I was a bit leery of returning to this new house, but when I walked in, it was home. Family photos line the hallways and shelves. And my dad's drums sit in a room full of Dallas Cowboys memorabilia and enough records and CDs to open a music store.

My favorite thing about going home is fishing with Daddy. When I was home recently, it rained most of the time, but as long as the rain wasn't accompanied by thunder and lightning, he was standing in the backyard throwing a line.

When my dad isn't working, you can find him fishing. Growing up, I often took this for granted because if I'm not hooking any, I get bored. I realize now how precious our time together is. Whenever I fish with Daddy, I think about Trace Adkins' song "Just Fishin' " because it really is always more than that.

Eternity wouldn't be enough time to go fishing with my Daddy. Living abroad has taught me to cherish the smallest of moments. But we really shouldn't have to be separated to remember how much our family loves us.

Though they live in different parts of the world, Amie always makes time for her dad.

We never talk about the really personal things, because I'm his girl and he's my daddy, ya know? But the thing I love most about him is how he reacted when he knew I was unhappy in our hometown. I'll never forget the moment he told me I should leave home.

That was painful, I know. And I see how it takes every ounce of his courage and strength to put me on a plane each time I leave. I can never thank him enough for giving me the push I needed.

I for sure take after my dad in many ways, and I'm thankful for each and every trait, even the bad habits. I love the bond we share, and although I can't remember every single moment, I have millions stored away.

I'm writing this to ask you all to remember and cherish your family every day, not just on the holidays. I promise to never get so wrapped up in this crazy life that I forget how to find my way home. ☀

Ruble, 86, "keeps going" by tending to his gardens and doing other activities.

Ruble in Motion

One man's gusto brings happiness to those around him.

BY MICHAEL MYERS *Greeneville, Tennessee*

I married a Norton girl 47 years ago and moved to Norton Road. On that happy day, Ruble Norton, my wife's cousin, became my friend and neighbor—the best anyone could have.

Ruble, a Korean War veteran, celebrated his 86th birthday recently. He has always lent a wise and helping hand.

In 2014, I was diagnosed with cancer. With that came radiation and chemo treatments. Our family, friends and neighbors were very helpful during that time, but soft-spoken Ruble was the alpha—a Good Samaritan extraordinaire. He did everything from keeping an eye on our house to planting flowers with his daughter around our mailbox to checking on us daily when we returned home.

The man never has a bad word to say about anyone and always has a smile on his face. Even though he has had a heart attack, he keeps plugging away. I recall Ruble's uncle saying, "If I ever sit down at my age, I may not be able to get back up. That's why I keep going."

It must be a Norton thing, because it rings true through Ruble today. He's always walking through the pastures, hoeing his garden, gathering produce, setting flowers—anything to keep moving. He can accidentally do more before breakfast than I can purposely do all day! We love him! ☀

You Are My Sunshine

These two have a special bond that brings work to a halt.

BY MELANIE HARVEY *Elliston, Virginia*

I was watching my 6-month-old granddaughter, Lila Sledd, on a beautiful, sunny day. My father-in-law, Frank Harvey, lives right next door to me. Knowing how much he loves to see his great-grandchildren, I took Lila over to visit with him. Frank was mowing hay in the field in front of our house. As soon as he saw us coming, he stopped the tractor to talk to little Lila. What a welcome break from putting up hay!

Frank has been farming his whole life. He grew up on a farm and is still working his 20-plus-acre farm today at age 87. He raises cattle and hogs and also has a couple of horses stabled there. He bales hay, plows and grows a garden, feeds and cares for the animals, and does the thousands of other jobs required on a farm.

I am forever grateful I caught this picture of Frank and Lila together as it captures the love between a man and his great-grandbaby. ☀

Great-Grandpa Frank and Lila share a tender moment on the farm.

Sweet Yesterdays

Catching tadpoles and playing in the barn beat churning butter every time.

BY PAT ENGLERT *Charlotte, North Carolina*

Some memories grow in farm fields; Pat with Grandma Etta.

Unforgettable images of time spent on my grandparents' farm in Mount Pleasant, North Carolina, fill my childhood memories with warmth.

The house stood in the curve of a narrow dirt road, with lush woods and rolling green pastures wrapped around it. The front porch's lazy white swing and rocking chairs invited a respite from the long day.

On hot summer days, we sat on the screened back porch and my grandmother Etta Elizabeth Cox taught me how to churn butter. Like Tom Sawyer whitewashing the fence, I soon learned that churning was boring, and I would run off to the weathered gray barn a short distance from the house.

When I got there I didn't bother to saddle my favorite chestnut horse. I just climbed on her back and rode through the apple orchard and pasture where the cows grazed until I reached the cool waters of the creek.

Catching tadpoles was a lot more fun than churning butter. And blackberries were plentiful along the creek. I ate them until my mouth turned purple.

When I visit there today, I love to walk in the places where I was so gloriously a child. I can still picture playing hide-and-seek with my three cousins in the barn and chasing sheep in the pasture.

During the winter, Grandma would pull me on her lap and rock me softly. The timeworn rocker squeaked, and the old fireplace spit and crackled as the flames licked the chimney.

As the fire died, my eyes grew heavy. Soon the sandman sprinkled sand in them, and Grandma gathered me softly in her warm arms, carried me up the stairs, tucked me in a bed with a warm feather mattress and covered me with patchwork quilts.

Cherishing my yesterdays gives my todays sweetness and love. ☀

Big John's Chili-Rubbed Ribs

PREP: 20 min. + chilling • **GRILL:** 1½ hours
MAKES: 10 servings

- 3 Tbsp. packed brown sugar
- 2 Tbsp. paprika
- 2 Tbsp. chili powder
- 3 tsp. ground cumin
- 2 tsp. garlic powder
- 1 tsp. salt
- 6 lbs. pork baby back ribs

GLAZE
- 1 cup reduced-sodium soy sauce
- 1 cup packed brown sugar
- ⅔ cup ketchup
- ⅓ cup lemon juice
- 1½ tsp. minced fresh gingerroot

1. Mix the first six ingredients; rub over ribs. Refrigerate, covered, 30 minutes.
2. Wrap the rib racks in large pieces of heavy-duty foil; seal tightly. Grill, covered, over indirect medium heat until tender, 1-1½ hours.
3. In a large saucepan, combine glaze ingredients; cook, uncovered, over medium heat until heated through and sugar is dissolved, 6-8 minutes, stirring occasionally.
4. Carefully remove ribs from foil. Place ribs over direct heat; brush with some of the glaze. Grill, covered, over medium heat until browned, 25-30 minutes, turning and brushing ribs occasionally with the remaining glaze.

1 serving: 486 cal., 26g fat (9g sat. fat), 98mg chol., 1543mg sod., 34g carb. (30g sugars, 1g fiber), 29g pro.

Triple Berry Shortcake

PREP: 25 min. • **BAKE:** 25 min. + cooling
MAKES: 15 servings

1	cup butter, softened
2	cups sugar
4	large eggs, room temperature
2	Tbsp. vanilla extract
3	cups all-purpose flour
1	tsp. baking powder
½	tsp. baking soda
½	tsp. salt
1	cup buttermilk

TOPPING

1½	cups fresh blueberries
1½	cups sliced fresh strawberries
1½	cups fresh raspberries
2	Tbsp. sugar
	Sweetened whipped cream, optional

1. Preheat oven to 350°. In a large bowl, cream butter and sugar until light and fluffy. Add eggs, one at a time, beating well after each addition. Beat in vanilla. In another bowl, whisk flour, baking powder, baking soda and salt; add to creamed mixture alternately with buttermilk, beating well after each addition.
2. Transfer batter to a greased 13x9-in. pan. Bake until a toothpick inserted in the center comes out clean, 25-30 minutes. Cool completely in pan on a wire rack.
3. For topping, in a large bowl, combine berries; add sugar and toss gently to coat. Serve with cake; top with whipped cream, if desired.

1 serving: 361 cal., 14g fat (8g sat. fat), 83mg chol., 301mg sod., 54g carb. (32g sugars, 2g fiber), 5g pro.

BLT Tortillas

TAKES: 15 min. • **MAKES:** 8 servings

½	cup mayonnaise
½	cup sour cream
2	Tbsp. ranch salad dressing mix
¼	tsp. crushed red pepper flakes
8	flour tortillas (8 in.), room temperature
16	cooked bacon strips
2 to 3	cups shredded lettuce
2	cups chopped seeded tomato
	Green and sweet red pepper strips, optional

Mix first four ingredients; spread onto tortillas. Top with remaining ingredients and roll up.

1 serving: 402 cal., 25g fat (7g sat. fat), 27mg chol., 890mg sod., 32g carb. (2g sugars, 2g fiber), 13g pro.

Watermelon & Spinach Salad

TAKES: 30 min. • **MAKES:** 8 servings

- ¼ cup rice vinegar or white wine vinegar
- 1 Tbsp. grated lime zest
- 2 Tbsp. lime juice
- 2 Tbsp. canola oil
- 4 tsp. minced fresh gingerroot
- 2 garlic cloves, minced
- ½ tsp. salt
- ¼ tsp. sugar
- ¼ tsp. pepper

SALAD
- 4 cups fresh baby spinach or arugula
- 3 cups cubed seedless watermelon
- 2 cups cubed cantaloupe
- 2 cups cubed English cucumber
- ½ cup chopped fresh cilantro
- 2 green onions, chopped

In a small bowl, whisk the first nine ingredients. In a large bowl, combine salad ingredients. Drizzle with dressing and toss to coat; serve immediately.

1 cup: 84 cal., 4g fat (0 sat. fat), 0 chol., 288mg sod., 13g carb. (10g sugars, 1g fiber), 1g pro.
Diabetic exchanges: 1 vegetable, 1 fat, ½ fruit.

Cilantro Lime Shrimp

TAKES: 30 min. • **MAKES:** 4 servings

- ⅓ cup chopped fresh cilantro
- 1½ tsp. grated lime zest
- ⅓ cup lime juice
- 1 jalapeno pepper, seeded and minced
- 2 Tbsp. olive oil
- 3 garlic cloves, minced
- ¼ tsp. salt
- ¼ tsp. ground cumin
- ¼ tsp. pepper
- 1 lb. uncooked shrimp (16-20 per lb.), peeled and deveined
  Lime slices

1. Mix first nine ingredients; toss with shrimp. Let stand 15 minutes.
2. Thread shrimp and lime slices onto four metal or soaked wooden skewers. Grill, covered, over medium heat until shrimp turn pink, 2-4 minutes per side.

1 serving: 167 cal., 8g fat (1g sat. fat), 138mg chol., 284mg sod., 4g carb. (1g sugars, 0 fiber), 19g pro.
Diabetic exchanges: 3 lean meat, 1½ fat.

Ginger Pound Cake S'mores

TAKES: 20 min.
MAKES: 8 servings

- **8 large marshmallows**
- **5 oz. bittersweet chocolate candy bars, broken into eight pieces**
- **8 tsp. crystallized ginger**
- **16 slices pound cake (¼ in. thick)**
- **3 Tbsp. butter, softened**

1. Cut each of the marshmallows lengthwise into four slices. Place the chocolate, four marshmallow slices and ginger on each of eight cake slices; top with remaining cake. Spread outsides of cake slices with butter.

2. Grill, covered, over medium heat until toasted, 1-2 minutes on each side.

1 s'more: 382 cal., 24g fat (13g sat. fat), 144mg chol., 272mg sod., 44g carb. (10g sugars, 2g fiber), 5g pro.

Pork Tenderloin with Three-Berry Salsa

PREP: 30 min. + standing · **COOK:** 25 min.
MAKES: 6 servings

- 1¼ **cups fresh or frozen blackberries (about 6 oz.), thawed and drained**
- 1¼ **cups fresh or frozen raspberries (about 6 oz.), thawed and drained**
- 1 **cup fresh or frozen blueberries (about 6 oz.), thawed**
- 1 **medium sweet red pepper, finely chopped**
- 1 **jalapeno pepper, seeded and minced**
- ½ **medium red onion, finely chopped**
- ¼ **cup lime juice**
- 3 **Tbsp. minced fresh cilantro**
- ¼ **tsp. salt**

PORK
- 2 **pork tenderloins (¾ lb. each), cut into ¾-in. slices**
- 1 **tsp. salt**
- ½ **tsp. pepper**
- 2 **Tbsp. olive oil, divided**
- ½ **cup white wine or chicken broth**
- 2 **shallots, thinly sliced**
- ½ **cup chicken broth**

1. Place the first five ingredients in a bowl; toss lightly to combine. Reserve 1 cup berry mixture for sauce. For salsa, gently stir onion, lime juice, cilantro and salt into remaining mixture; let stand 30 minutes.

2. Meanwhile, sprinkle pork with salt and pepper. In a large skillet, heat 1 Tbsp. oil over medium-high heat. Add half of the pork and cook until a thermometer inserted in pork reads 145°, 2-4 minutes on each side. Remove from pan. Repeat with remaining pork and oil.

3. In same pan, add white wine, shallots and the reserved berry mixture, stirring to loosen browned bits from pan. Bring to a boil; cook until liquid is reduced to 1 Tbsp., 4-6 minutes. Stir in the chicken stock; cook until shallots are tender, about 5 minutes longer, stirring occasionally. Return pork to pan; heat through. Serve with salsa.

3 oz. cooked pork with ⅔ cup salsa and 3 Tbsp. sauce: 239 cal., 9g fat (2g sat. fat), 64mg chol., 645mg sod., 15g carb. (7g sugars, 5g fiber), 25g pro.
Diabetic exchanges: 3 lean meat, ½ starch, ½ fruit.

Basil Tomato Tart

PREP: 20 min. • **BAKE:** 20 min. • **MAKES:** 8 servings

> Pastry for a single-crust pie (9 in.)

- 1½ cups shredded part-skim mozzarella cheese, divided
- 5 to 6 fresh plum tomatoes
- 1 cup loosely packed fresh basil leaves
- 4 garlic cloves
- ½ cup mayonnaise
- ¼ cup grated Parmesan cheese
- ⅛ tsp. pepper

1. Roll pastry to fit a 9-in. tart pan or pie plate; place in pan. Do not prick. Line pastry shell with a double thickness of heavy-duty foil.

2. Bake at 450° for 5 minutes. Remove foil; bake 8 minutes more. Remove from the oven. Reduce heat to 375°. Sprinkle ½ cup mozzarella over the hot crust.

3. Cut each tomato into eight wedges; remove seeds. Arrange over cheese.

4. In a food processor, process the basil and garlic until coarsely chopped; sprinkle over tomatoes.

5. Combine mayonnaise, Parmesan, pepper and the remaining mozzarella; spoon over basil. Bake, uncovered, until the cheese is browned and bubbly, 20-25 minutes.

1 piece: 345 cal., 27g fat (12g sat. fat), 47mg chol., 413mg sod., 19g carb. (2g sugars, 1g fiber), 8g pro.

Stuffed Grilled Zucchini

PREP: 25 min. • **GRILL:** 10 min. • **MAKES:** 4 servings

- 4 medium zucchini
- 5 tsp. olive oil, divided
- 2 Tbsp. finely chopped red onion
- ¼ tsp. minced garlic
- ½ cup dry bread crumbs
- ½ cup shredded part-skim mozzarella cheese
- 1 Tbsp. minced fresh mint
- ½ tsp. salt
- 3 Tbsp. grated Parmesan cheese

1. Cut zucchini in half lengthwise; scoop out pulp, leaving ¼-in. shells. Brush with 2 tsp. oil; set aside. Chop pulp.

2. In a large skillet, saute pulp and onion in remaining oil. Add garlic; cook 1 minute longer. Add bread crumbs; cook and stir until golden brown, about 2 minutes.

3. Remove from the heat. Stir in the mozzarella cheese, mint and salt. Spoon into zucchini shells. Sprinkle with Parmesan cheese.

4. Grill, covered, over medium heat until zucchini is tender, 8-10 minutes.

2 stuffed zucchini halves: 186 cal., 10g fat (3g sat. fat), 11mg chol., 553mg sod., 17g carb. (4g sugars, 3g fiber), 9g pro.

HANDCRAFTED WITH LOVE

Dish Designs

Give a set of secondhand
plates a new look.

WHAT YOU'LL NEED

- Fabric
- Secondhand glass plates
- Dishwasher-safe decoupage glue
- Scissors
- Foam brush

DIRECTIONS

1. Cut a square piece of fabric 2 in. wider
   than plate circumference.
2. Using a foam brush, apply decoupage
   glue to bottom of plate.
3. Lay fabric, print side down, on top of
   the glue, pressing to adhere to plate.
   Smooth fabric down with foam brush
   and apply a coat of decoupage glue
   over the fabric. Let dry overnight.
4. Using scissors, trim fabric to plate
   edge. Apply two or three more coats
   of decoupage glue on the bottom of
   plate, sealing fabric.

Picture Perfect

Go to great lengths and set off your snaps in a DIY frame made of old advertising rulers.

WHAT YOU'LL NEED
- 11x14-in. photo frame
- Corkboard sheet
- Hardboard
- Old rulers or yardsticks
- Scissors
- Saw
- Finish nailer
- Hot glue gun

DIRECTIONS
1. Remove the backing, glass and mat from photo frame. Cut a piece of a corkboard sheet to the frame size and fit it into the frame.
2. Using a saw, cut a piece of hardboard large enough to cover the back of the frame. Nail in place with a finish nailer.
3. Measure and mark a 5½x7½-in. or 4½x6½-in. opening in the middle of the corkboard for the picture.
4. Cut old rulers or yardsticks in a variety of lengths, and fit the pieces around the opening for the photo, placing them both horizontally and vertically. Continue cutting and fitting pieces until the entire frame is covered, and glue into place using a hot glue gun.

Cute as a Button

Tame unruly tablecloths at your next picnic with a string of decorative fasteners.

WHAT YOU'LL NEED
- Fishing line
- Glass or other heavy buttons
- Badge clip
- Scissors

DIRECTIONS
1. Cut a length of fishing line and tie one end to a button; this will be the bottom of the strand. Continue to string other buttons on the line until the desired length and look is achieved.
2. Tie the top end of the line to a badge clip. Hang a few on the hem of a tablecloth, and let the wind blow.

Autumn

Brilliant fall foliage lines
the shoreline of Perkins
Pond in New Hampshire.
PHOTO BY PAUL REZENDES

APPRECIATE THE SIMPLE PLEASURES

THE GOOD LIFE

'God's Hand Was in It All'

This ranch family found their happily ever after with
horses, cattle and over 300 acres of gorgeous country.

BY SARAH LEA BOWMAN *Olathe, Colorado*

There's a difference between living and living well. And sometimes that difference means setting aside your dreams and fully embracing the life that God has given you.

Born and raised in western Colorado, I have always loved the outdoors and animals. Though we moved too often for me to have animals of my own besides cats and gerbils, I had a chance to start riding horses when I was 12.

Three times a week my parents took me to a stable where I signed up for lessons and began competing.

Ever since, I have poured myself into learning about horses and improving my riding and training skills.

By the time I was 15, I managed to save up enough money to purchase a 2-year-old quarter horse filly from a breeder friend of my mine. That horse taught me so much. Thanks to lots of instruction, I trained her myself and we competed together in 4-H and open shows.

I had one goal in mind, and that was to become a professional trainer. So when I graduated from high school, I chose a college that offered a degree in horse

Andrew Bowman checks on the cows with the San Juan Mountains in the distance.

While fixing up their home, the couple started a business to board and train horses. Sarah finds joy living on their land and through faith and family.

training, which gave me the opportunity to do an internship with a top-notch reining horse trainer, Steve Schwartzenberger.

The next year, I married my cowboy, Andrew Bowman. While he loves working horses and looking after cattle, he is also a good mechanic and welder who can fix almost anything.

After a time of working together on a large cattle ranch, we decided to build a house on his parents' land. The Bow K Ranch consists of 365 acres of sloping irrigated hayfields and grassy pastures surrounded by steep barren hills.

Circled by a life-giving irrigation canal, the ranch backs up to miles of cactus-covered plateaus and pinyon pines, with the ragged snowcapped San Juan Mountains in the distance. Just behind the ranch there is a deep canyon that contains evidence of bygone times, such as a Native American flint cave and a huge petroglyph-covered rock.

We bought an old farmhouse that was a few miles down the road and had it moved to the family ranch. I've always loved historic houses; it was a dream come true being able to get one placed here.

Andrew then built a basement underneath it and completed the necessary remodeling. A major project, God's hand was in it all.

From the dining room window, nearly the whole ranch is in view, as well as Grand Mesa, the largest flat-topped mountain in the world. Horses graze in the pasture closest to the house, and cattle roam over the remainder of the ranch. Nearby pens house our goats and ducks. A path winds to a small garden.

As our farmhouse was coming together, we started our horse training business, offering colt starting, working with problem horses, giving riding lessons and boarding horses.

I have always done a little artwork in between riding. Naturally my main subject has been horses, though I also enjoy dogs, and currently I prefer doing still-life drawings of saddles and boots. Mostly I work with graphite or colored pencils.

Eight years after starting the business, we do more boarding than training, which allows me to spend extra time raising our 4-year-old daughter, Kyanne. Seeing her delight in animals and the outdoors brings me joy. Nothing warms my heart more than when she looks out across the beautiful mountains in awe and whispers, "Thank you, Jesus!"

Kyanne loves riding her miniature horse and helping out with the border collie puppies we raise. Part of her daily routine includes going with me to milk the goats, gather the eggs and walk the dogs. She carries hay to her horse and helps bring veggies up from the garden.

When Andrew isn't feeding the horses or caring for our growing herd of Gelbvieh cattle, he helps with a cowboy church that puts on summer camps for the rodeo youth of the area. Andrew also joins in with the band most Sundays.

While training and competing have been put on the back burner for now, I have come to appreciate the beauty in the life God has given me. The ranch that my family calls home and the beautiful mountain that we run our cows on are the most incredible country I could ever ask for. ☀

A Peaceful Adjustment

With two small boys to raise, we left our city life behind and headed for the country.

BY JACKIE HOSTETLER *Edgerton, Kansas*

We used to live in a busy suburb of Kansas City. I awoke to the steady hum of traffic on the road, mere feet from our front door. Car alarms and sirens lulled me to sleep for years. I ran to the market on a daily basis to purchase our groceries; a quick dinner was just a block away, with no planning or preparation needed.

Nothing is far when you live in the city. Three gas stations were within a stone's throw, and my house was just 5 miles from the hospital where I brought two strapping boys into the world—Hayden, now 6, and William, now 4. What do you do when you have two such boys to raise?

For my husband, Ryan, and me, the answer was to leave the city, with our small boys in tow, and come to the country.

At our new home, about an hour south, the quiet was disconcerting to my ears at first, but immediately soothing to my soul. It took many weeks to get used to the calm. But it was a peaceful adjustment.

We open our windows wide in the evening to let the moonlight shine in, with curtains billowing in the breeze. Our shades are always open. No curious eyes to keep out, only nature's beauty to let in. Gone is the nightly song of sirens, never to return.

Miles from conveniences, we now plan meals on a calendar. We grow our boys on squash from the garden, eggs from our prize hen, Snowy, and her nine sisters—though none quite as special as Snowy—and canned goods stocked weeks in advance. One day soon we will all have a hard lesson to learn involving our two cattle, Murray and Willis, who live in the barn and moo contentedly.

The occasional trip to a nearby town for an ice cream cone is always a treat. Two boys, now sticky from head to toe, return home just in time to acquire a layer of dirt on top of the sticky. The bathwater is as dark as the creek that trickles beyond the pasture.

Clean boys emerge from the tub, backs brown from afternoons in the sun. The clean will last only for the hours they are in bed. Their feet will be dirty again before breakfast is served.

When we first moved out here, I commuted to Kansas City for work, but that didn't last very long. Now I am an elementary schoolteacher in the rural school district that my boys attend, and I'm so happy to be there.

Unpaved roads, ruddy and washed out by rains, bring me home. Though it is high summer, roadside patches of grass and groves of trees appear to be covered in a silvery frost. It's gravel dust that creates a delicate patina on everything within settling distance. The effect

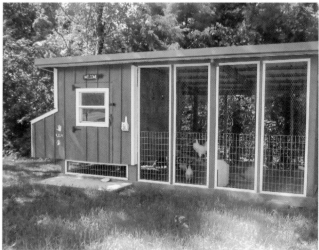

In the country, the family has room to roam and explore. The chicken coop includes a mailbox so the boys can write letters to the hens.

I gaze upon the endless horizon with a tinge of doubt. What a large piece of prairie for two small boys. Are we safe? Is this right?

is simultaneously beautiful and eerie. This fake "frost" will be washed away, though, with the next rain and accumulate again in the heat of the afternoon. The cycle continues until the true frost comes with the changing of the seasons.

With frost comes a vastness that is not felt by one in the other seasons. The trees become bare. I can see land for miles around our home, which was previously obscured by leaves and tall grass. It can raise concerns. I gaze upon the endless horizon with a tinge of doubt. What a large piece of prairie for two small boys. Are we safe? Is this right?

Doubt is replaced with joy as I see pink noses and pink cheeks. Small, mittened hands furiously store nuts, twigs and countless other treasures in an abandoned lean-to. Each item has a purpose, known only to these two small curators. They are aware of the land, aware of its gifts. This is right.

Just as my boys store away their treasures, I store my most precious memories. William, my smallest boy, swinging from a tree as leaves and sunlight create shadows that fall on his face and hair: The swirls of light mingle with his curls; his beauty merges with the beauty of the land around him.

My oldest boy, Hayden, still quite little, is silhouetted against the sky, his sturdy legs and booted feet stomping the ground with glee. A long stick navigates the path while a spotted dog bounces behind. It is a perfect picture of a happy child.

We live in the country among cherries, wild daisies, wildlife and birds and, most importantly, our two little boys, who won't be little for long. ☀

William and his big brother, Hayden, play and share secrets on their daddy's trailer.

Little House on the Ranch

An idyllic spot of land in Northern California becomes a dream homestead.

BY MARY HEFFERNAN *Fort Jones, California*

My husband, Brian, and I spent years dreaming of having some land in the country where we could spend weekends and let our kids run free in the dirt and the sunshine. We both have deep agricultural roots and a passion for small towns, small businesses and family-centered food. In 2013, as we were living in Silicon Valley, California, and working hard in the business world, we found the historic Sharps Gulch Ranch in far northern California.

Brian and I knew we'd located the land of our dreams, and we purchased it to use as a weekend getaway. But it didn't take long for us to realize we also had a calling to a new lifestyle. Soon after buying the land, we packed up our urban lives and moved up here to raise pastured animals and share them with the world.

We are Five Marys Farms. Brian named the farm for our four young daughters and me. Each daughter is named Mary after our aunts and grandmothers on both sides of the family. MaryFrances, also known as Francie, is 9 and loves dogs and the veterinary aspects of the ranch. MaryMarjorie, or Maisie, is 8 and can usually be found in her ranch clothes working alongside her dad. MaryJane, or JJ, is 6 and just adores tending to the

Four of the five Marys in their Sunday best; colorful pumpkins and other squash brighten the front porch of a neighbor.

sweet baby lambs. MaryTeresa—Tessa—is 4, and she's the spunky-but-tough baby of the family. Together, we proudly work the ranch with Brian.

Our girls are strong, self-reliant and helpful in the ranch's daily operations. They ride their horses or four-wheelers to help us move cattle. They collect fresh eggs, care for sick lambs and bottle-feed newborn calves in our living room. When they're not ranching, they attend a lovely small public school just 5 miles down the road.

We live in a tiny, 780-square-foot cabin heated by our wood stove. We cut firewood together every Sunday, and we're so grateful to sit around a warm and comforting fire on chilly evenings.

When we first moved here, the girls shared a double bed. After two years, I got out my hammer and nails and converted the attic space into a loft-style bedroom. Each girl is happy to have her own bed now, and they don't mind sharing a room. We cook most of our meals together, and we eat at a little dining table in the corner of our cozy house.

Every day, our family of six canvasses the ranch's 1,800 acres. We feed our many animals; check waterers; sort, vaccinate and brand our cattle; help deliver new litters of piglets; and herd our sheep into

GIRLS, HOUSE: MARY HEFFERNAN; COWS: JOY PROUTY

Soon after buying the land, we packed up our urban lives and moved up here to raise pastured animals and share them with the world.

Mary Heffernan and daughter MaryJane herd cows onto a greener pasture, part of a rotational grazing plan.

greener pastures. Our 400 acres of irrigated pastures are bordered by the beautiful Scott River, which is a protected coho salmon habitat. Cattle and sheep graze on our grass pastures, and we reserve the four big alfalfa fields for growing winter feed. We grow enough to support our herds throughout the winter, feeding more than 80 bales to the cattle and sheep each day during the coldest months of the year.

We raise all-natural Black Angus beef, grass-fed Navajo-Churro lamb, Gloucestershire Old Spots heritage pigs and farm-fresh eggs in a rainbow of colors. Most of our animals are born on our ranch and live a pretty idyllic life here. We keep bees and produce wildflower honey. We tan sheepskin hides. We also make spice rubs, seasonings and various other products that we sell on our website. We sell every cut of beef, pork and lamb directly to customers all across the U.S. We pack these cuts on blocks of dry ice in insulated boxes and ship them out three days a week from our farm store in downtown Fort Jones. Thanks to social media, our customers feel a connection to our family and our ranch. Online we share the ups and downs, the good and the bad, and everything that happens on a real working ranch.

When the work is complete, we explore the ranch's mountainsides and sloping vistas on horseback or on foot. Our cattle and sheep graze on pastures that sit at an elevation of 2,800 feet, and it's nearly 1,600 feet of gain to the highest peak on our land. We ride ATVs up the mountainside to a saddle in the ridgeline that offers 360-degree views of the Marble Mountains and the Trinity Alps.

We face challenges, but that's just part of ranching. There are fluctuations in the commodities markets, health issues and crop problems, and the weather is unpredictable, but we love the satisfaction and purpose that this life provides. We end each day on our serene front porch. Brian and I sit in our Adirondack chairs while the girls pile onto an old couch. From there, we watch the animals bed down for the night. Then we fall into our own beds, dog-tired. ☀

MaryTeresa Heffernan, the youngest Mary, cuddles a lamb abandoned by its mother and chases hens while collecting eggs. The girls get to experience everything that happens on their family's working ranch.

Eye in the Sky

These birds of prey answer the call to keep pests away.

BY MOLLY JASINSKI *Milwaukee, Wisconsin*

When it comes to keeping ranches, vineyards and orchards free of pesky bird species, there's a new set of raptors in town.

Kathleen Tigan, owner of Tactical Avian Predators Inc., works with a crew of five falcons, a hawk, an owl and a trusty pack of dogs. Together they scare off would-be pests from all kinds of agricultural land, as well as outdoor dining areas and other places nuisance birds gather.

Starlings, crows and ravens can destroy valuable crops overnight. Farmers and ranchers hire Kathleen, who is a licensed falconer, to patrol the skies and keep trouble away. It's known as abatement falconry, an alternative to such traditional preventative measures as poison, noisemakers and fireworks.

The main objective of abatement falconry is not to hurt the nuisance birds—it's simply to ward them off.

Stryker, a male saker falcon, prepares to cast off from Kathleen Tigan's glove for a flight.

Because a group of 20 or so starlings can easily expand into thousands overnight, prevention is key.

Kathleen says her birds are up for the challenge. "Who [better] to remove a pest than something that, by nature, hunts pest birds?"

Every day looks different for an abatement falconer, but Kathleen says a typical day finds her working the acreage at one of her contracted properties, which span northern Nevada and California, keeping an eye out for nuisance birds.

"There are a lot of ways to do abatement falconry," Kathleen says. "Every job is different. You always have to think outside the box and come up with a new plan."

Once Kathleen spots a flock of problem birds, it's showtime. She quietly parks her truck nearby and determines which one of her fierce fliers is best for the task. Kathleen often employs the hawk for tighter spaces, such as between silos and buildings, while a

Zsa Zsa, a female peregrine falcon, performs a flyover.

falcon is better suited for wide-open fields. She'll call on Louise, her Eurasian eagle-owl, for tasks that require the bird's powerful presence. "I use her like a big plastic owl," Kathleen says, referring to the kind that gardeners use. While working under contract with the famed Pebble Beach Golf Links, Kathleen perched Louise near the 18th green. Her presence was enough to scare off unwanted birds from the area, including nearby dining venues.

Once she decides which raptor should fly, Kathleen holds the bird on her gloved hand before releasing it. She also turns loose a few dogs to help stir up the troublemakers and send them fleeing into the sky.

From there, the hawk or falcon will start "hazing." A raptor in hazing mode acts as if it's hunting. Though Kathleen's birds have been trained to refrain from attacking, they act like predators, so the prey species follow their instincts to flee.

Kathleen says falcons have a unique quality when entering hunt mode—they change their flying pattern to indicate they mean business: "They start to fly faster with a more intentional wingbeat than normal."

Once Kathleen determines that the problem has been chased away, she calls her bird back by blowing a whistle and swinging a lure. She rewards the bird with a chunk of quail and then repeats the ritual to make sure

I'm one of a small percentage of people whose passion turned into a career.

potential invaders notice the raptors. "I am often asked how it works, and I say, 'It seems like magic,'" she says.

Kathleen's journey began at an early age. She remembers loving animals as a child, but her passion for falconry took off when she got a job at the Columbia Gorge Discovery Center & Museum in The Dalles, Oregon, where she became involved with the raptor education program.

In 2009, she signed herself up for a falconry class in California, and that's where she met her future husband, James. Years later, she took over the falconry business he'd started.

"I owe James everything for the opportunity to have the coolest job and life," she says.

Now she's a one-woman show, helping customers safely avoid large crop losses.

A big factor in choosing abatement falconry is economic, Kathleen says. Vineyards will often buy netting to keep starlings away, which can be costly for large operations.

"I know of entire vineyards that did not harvest a single grape due to starlings," Kathleen says. "A very prominent winery lost 250 acres of cabernet grapes in a three-day period—a total loss for the year."

The management at Hahn Family Wines in Soledad, California, hired Kathleen and her raptors 10 years ago after realizing it was a cheaper solution than netting. Now the vineyard is a regular customer.

The winery especially relies on Kathleen when the grapes begin to ripen every year. As the starch in the grapes changes to sugar, the fruit becomes an appealing snack to a variety of birds. Starlings, in particular, are problematic. Their fondness for grape seeds not only damages crops, but creates a mess.

Kathleen recently began work with a beef ranch in Nevada that is also growing rye, oats and hay. Abatement falconry helps keep pest birds from interfering with the ranch's crops.

Falconry requires a lot of time, patience and money to keep up the required licenses, but Kathleen considers herself lucky.

"I'm one of a small percentage of people whose passion turned into a career," she says. "I am self-employed, don't work standard hours in an office setting and spend most days surrounded by animals. My job is heaven on earth." ☀

Christina Pfenning Craig contributed to this story.

Beebe, a male saker falcon, takes off to chase starlings at Hahn Family Wines in the Santa Lucia Highlands of Soledad, California. The vineyard relies on Kathleen's company to keep grapes safe on the vines.

The Straw Sculptors

Our farm community works as a team to turn big bales into amazing artwork.

BY KATHY CORGATELLI NEVILLE *Idaho Falls, Idaho*

A few years ago, Darla Hoff painted a pumpkin face onto a round straw bale to advertise her U-pick pumpkin patch at Al and Karen Goldman's farm in Idaho Falls. While Darla has stopped growing pumpkins, the annual tradition of straw bale art lives on at the farm and has grown to involve a group of friends and neighbors.

Once Darla comes up with an idea, the team gets right to work. Past creations have included an owl, Minions, dueling tractors, Thomas the Tank Engine and a lovable teddy bear.

The impressive public art has become quite an attraction. "People who drive by seem to get a kick out of it," Al says.

When Darla, her daughter Savannah, and Darla's sister DeAnne Hoots painted Minion faces on three of the round straw bales, these bright yellow critters were the talk of the town. The Minion display was the site of a wedding proposal and children's field trips, and it also lured many picture-takers and admirers.

"We all picked a different face and chose a straw bale," Darla says. "It was my favorite display."

The giant teddy bear was Karen's favorite. "His great big smile just made me happy," she says.

Dueling tractors have since replaced the Minions in Darla's affections. For these, Al, a loyal John Deere

> ## The farm's annual straw bale art projects have become a way for everyone to celebrate the end of another growing season.

owner, baled round straw bales in two different sizes—smaller ones for the tractor's front tires and larger ones for the rear.

Large square bales made up the bodies. Jerry Kienlen used his equipment to arrange the bales in the shape of two tractors.

Then it was time to bring the tractors to life. Karen and her daughter, Lana Hedrick, secured some green paint from Bingham County Implement in Blackfoot, and Steven Longhurst, a devoted Case equipment owner, got some red paint from Pioneer Equipment in Idaho Falls.

Darla's husband, James, sprayed the entire creation with a paint gun. For the finishing touches, Steven

Karen, Al and Darla design a new creation each fall. People enjoyed the Minions so much they took photos with them.

Many helpers came together to build a teddy bear and dueling tractors.
Colors on the bales are applied with a spray gun.

donated two shiny exhaust stacks, and Al and Karen salvaged two steering wheels from their farm parts stash.

The farm's annual straw bale art projects have become a way for everyone to celebrate the end of another growing season. "It's just something fun to do together after harvest," Al says.

Generations of these families have planted potatoes, grains and alfalfa in this fertile soil. Raised on the farms they now cultivate, they grew up together as their elders did before them.

"This neighborhood has always been close," says Jane Hoff, Darla's mother-in-law.

It helps that Al and Karen are truly super neighbors. Every year they grow about 2 acres of corn to give away. Al's dad started the tradition 20 years ago, and Al and Karen have kept it going. Anyone can pick some; the Hoffs will even deliver.

And during long Idaho winters, everyone congregates at the farm, where fresh coffee and cookies are served like clockwork at 10 a.m. and again at 3 p.m.

The next straw bale creation theme is Straw Wars. Without a doubt, the force will be with the team. And all eyes will be on Al and Karen's farm as their creation takes shape. ☀

SCRAPBOOK

On a fall getaway, my wife and I traveled to Lancaster County, Pennsylvania.
Boy, did the apples smell and taste great at this farm stand!
SCOTT HARRELL *Glen Allen, Virginia*

It was a rare treat to be the only visitor at Cucumber
Falls in Pennsylvania's Ohiopyle State Park.
CHARLOTTE PLETCHER *Somerset, Pennsylvania*

Our girls jumped into the middle of a leaf pile with their beloved pet goat. Fall is the perfect time for cuddles, and this is my all-time favorite autumn photo.
BRITNEY DENMAN *Hornbeak, Tennessee*

Mark Griffin Jr. and Arron Ramey make music at Chattanooga's Oktoberfest.
DONNA MULLINS *Ooltewah, Tennessee*

Half Way Farm in Chautauqua County decorates this old wagon every fall. Makes me smile every time!
JUDY WRODA *Ashville, New York*

A herd of cattle takes a break from keeping an eye on the autumn scenery in Stowe, Vermont.
PHOTO BY DONLAND/SHUTTERSTOCK

Fall is on its way to this lovely farm in Lebanon County near my home.
CAROL JACOBS NORWOOD *Myerstown, Pennsylvania*

I had to laugh when I saw my cat, Morris, blending right in with the autumn decorations!
LINDA SELFRIDGE *Ridgefield, Washington*

My son, Billy, loves his daughter, Ariel.
BONNIE POTOCZNY
Farmington, West Virginia

Colorado's glowing foliage caught my eye in a meadow of the San Juan National Forest, between the historic mining towns of Durango and Silverton.
ARNOLD BAUMFALK *St. Helens, Oregon*

Corn shocks dry in the warm autumn sunshine
on an Amish farm near Kidron, Ohio.
PHOTO BY AMERICA/ALAMY STOCK PHOTO

While taking pictures for our parents' anniversary present, my brother, Ethan, leaned against a hay bale and stuck a piece of straw in his mouth.
REBECCA FINCHUM *Strawberry Plains, Tennessee*

This was a perfect fall day. Cool, crisp temperatures, high school football, tall corn and a sweet red barn.
KRIS KLINGAMAN *Fairbank, Iowa*

I saw this young sharp-shinned hawk from my kitchen window.
JACQUELINE MILBURN *Boyce, Virginia*

Across the Midwest each fall, combines gobble up golden fields of soybeans.
PHOTO BY JOE MAMER PHOTOGRAPHY/ALAMY STOCK PHOTO

Our daughter, Addison, visits horses
when she sees her grandparents.
MIKE AND TRICIA JAGER
Lynden, Washington

Colorful leaves perfectly framed the Glade Creek Grist Mill
at Babcock State Park in West Virginia.
RAYMOND MASSEY *Sherburne, New York*

This charming New England farm looks like the ideal spot to buy a pumpkin for the porch.
PHOTO BY FRANK VETERE/ALAMY STOCK PHOTO

Upon Sadie Mae's first experience with pumpkins, she quickly picked one out to be her jack-o'-lantern.
TAMI GINGRICH *Middlefield, Ohio*

When my husband and I pulled into the parking lot of C.R. Lapp's Family Restaurant in Quarryville, we saw this field of pumpkins. The farmers had two tractor-trailers full by the time we finished breakfast.
JOANN L. FUIR *Ronks, Pennsylvania*

A windmill in Colorado stands tall as sunlight bursts through the clouds.
PHOTO BY BRAD NICOL/ALAMY STOCK PHOTO

The annual trip to the pumpkin patch with our nephew's family was extra special this year. Little Evy got to bring along her new baby brother, Liam.
KAREN CHRISTMAN *Amston, Connecticut*

Our son, Makai, helped Daddy collect firewood during our last family camping trip before Utah's American Fork Canyon closed for the winter.
ANNIE THOMSON *Provo, Utah*

My grandsons, Jack and Eli, live on our farm, where we host a corn maze and a pumpkin patch.
On this day, I spotted them running with glee to the hayride.
MARY JANE McDONALD *Zanesville, Ohio*

Though he's just a boy, Peyton has a love for farming.
Look into his eyes—you can see a future farmer.
LORRI MILTON *Friend, Nebraska*

American goldfinches use broomcorn as
a perch while waiting for the feeders.
JAMES PRUTILPAC
Morgantown, West Virginia

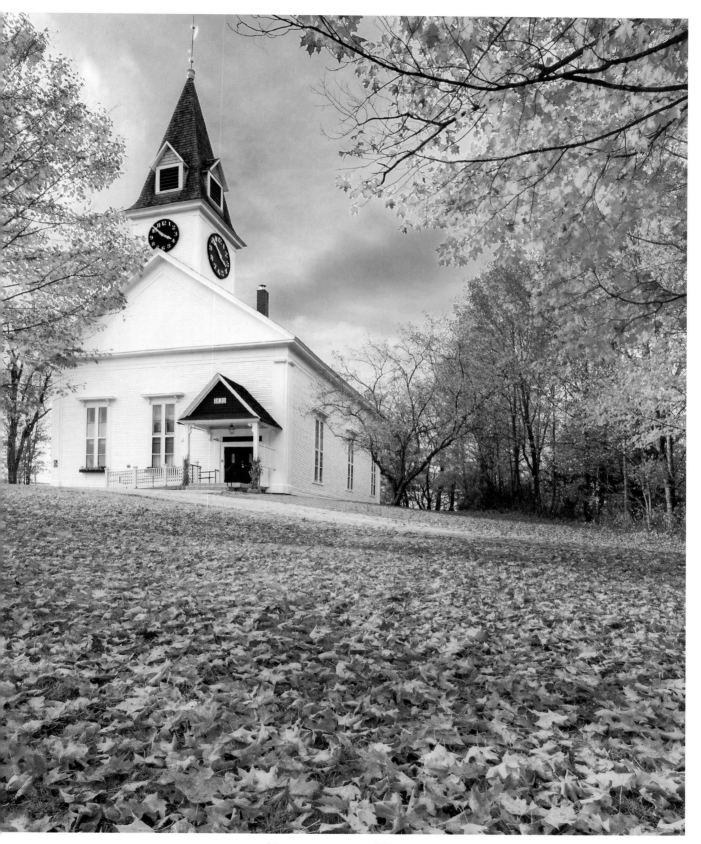

**A carpet of leaves welcomes visitors to a meeting house
in Sugar Hill, New Hampshire.
PHOTO BY PAT & CHUCK BLACKLEY**

HEART & SOUL

A Working Day

Twice a year, family and friends saddle up for a ranching tradition.

BY KELLY G. WILLIAMS *Lexington, Virginia*

Kelly and her brother-in-law Warren separate calves from cows.

On a cattle ranch, a working day is an explosion of the senses. Hot, sweaty horses; barking dogs; grime and mud; skittering calves and noisy cows calling for their young. All the laughing, yelling and genial camaraderie adds to the chaos and fun.

Everyone helps, and as each year passes, it remains thrilling to watch the slow movement of a herd pushed forward by the subtle momentum created by men and women on horseback. It is a beautiful dance performed by the rider, the horse and the herd.

My husband, Mike, and I bring in our entire herd twice a year for shots, tagging and record keeping. We bring them in at other times as well, but these two big working days are the most important for the health, well-being and continuity of our herd and our operation.

Friends and family come with horses in tow to help us celebrate another successful season on our ranch, which is in the mountains outside of Lexington. Our help consists of Mike's brother Warren and his girlfriend, Angela, plus a group of our friends and their kids.

My oldest daughter, Ashley, is a small-animal veterinarian, and when she shows up, she usually brings along a vet tech or two who are in need of large-animal experience.

In any roundup, when the herd is contained, the work begins. Usually we start by separating the dry cows—the ones without calves—and run them through the chute, a close-fitting metal cage consisting of a head catch and a body squeeze that restricts the cows' movement. The chute holds the cows in place for vaccinations and worming. Once the dry cows have been doctored and turned back out, the fun begins.

Try to imagine how you would feel if you were suddenly separated from your small child in a grocery store, airport or shopping mall. Panic sets in, and as a parent, all that matters is recovering your child. Now multiply that panic by the number of cows (weighing 1,400 pounds each) as they all try to stay with their calves during the separation process.

We work hard to run our pen quietly, keeping it as stress-free as possible for our animals, but despite our best intentions, things can get wild. The presence of so many horses, riders and a bunch of people on foot really ramps up the energy. Mayhem ensues: cows charging; calves skittering in all directions; horses snorting, running and jumping as everyone tries to move the cows into one pen and the calves into another as quickly as possible.

I live for the excitement of it all. I have lots of wild stories related to working cattle—perfect ones to share over a campfire after a long day. Over time, these stories ultimately grow in stature, creating a great cowboy tall tale.

When all the work is finished and the cows and calves are paired back up, happily grazing, it is time for the day to wind down with a great meal. Mike and I couldn't do this hard work without our family and friends, so this is our way of thanking them for their help, sweat and support.

I have lots of wild stories related to working cattle—perfect ones to share over a campfire after a long day.

I have a sense of pride knowing our cattle are taken care of and ready for a new season. It's hard work, filled with challenges and danger, but I believe what we do is vital to the survival of our nation. To me, feeding people is a noble pursuit. The day-to-day work has its hurdles, but we persevere because we are passionate about what we do.

As a teen, I wanted a big life. I wanted to be wealthy, but in a shallow sort of way that wasn't fulfilling. Now I have a bigger, wealthier life in an important, spiritual way. I have learned the best things in life are not things. Happiness is an ongoing journey, and most of the things I might worry about today won't matter tomorrow. Living in the moment puts the struggles of each day into a positive perspective. There's no better way to share your life than with the people you love and the animals you care for. ☀

After being immunized the mother-calf pairs are reunited.

The Art of Kindness

His caring heart fills a truck bed and the surrounding area with beauty.

BY SONJA STEPHENS *Mesa, Arizona*

As a farmer's daughter and an artist, I look for alluring farm subjects when I travel. While driving a country road in American Fork, Utah, I came to the Carlisle Fruit Farm and saw a sight for my creative eyes: a run-down 1942 International truck with wood carvings of enormous fall pumpkins on the bed. I grabbed my camera and began taking pictures. With the stunning snowcapped mountains in the background, I imagined the painting I would create.

Curious, I asked if I could meet the master "pumpkin carver." I located him, a man named Bob Carlisle, just down the road. He was restoring and modernizing his 1860 pioneer cabin, which he said was the first one built in the area. He also told me he'd carved the pumpkins out of various tree stumps from the property. He told me stories about his life, about the hardships he had endured and his passion for helping the homeless. In the past, he said, he had used a farmhouse on the orchard's land as a temporary safe haven for homeless men while they got back on their feet.

Making a positive impact runs in Bob's family. His parents, Neil and LouCille Carlisle, were longtime residents of Alpine, Utah. Upon digging a deep well to irrigate their land, they hit an aquifer that, purchased by the city in 1996, still supplies water to the area. Carlisle Memorial Park exists to honor them. The park was an Eagle Scout project, and Bob's parents' names are etched into a memorial stone there.

Three months after that first visit, I returned to Bob's cabin. It was beautifully restored. I slipped inside and hung the painting on a wall; it just seemed to belong. When Bob came in the front door, he saw it and, with grateful tears in his eyes, graciously thanked me. I thanked him for being such an inspiration and an example to so many. ☀

Sonja's painting of an abandoned truck was inspired by a heartwarming story of generosity.

We Take Care of Our Own

*The folks in our small town knew just what to do when
my family needed a helping hand.*

BY PATTI CLARK *Concord, California*

My baby brother came into the
world two weeks after I started
high school. At 14, I was the
oldest of three and hoped this
baby wasn't going to rain on my
parade very much. Being a big sister again just
wasn't part of my plan.

But two minutes after Keith was born, Mom
had a stroke. The doctor told Dad if it had
happened during the delivery the stroke likely
would have killed them both.

When Dad came home, he said the future was
uncertain because Mom might not survive. I was
so scared when he pulled me onto his lap and said,
"Well, little girl, looks like we've got a baby to
raise." My strong father was clearly petrified. He was
unintentionally leaning on me to help him through it.

But I need not have worried. Keith's arrival brought
out the very best in Wayland, Michigan. The old saying
"we take care of our own" was never better illustrated.

A young couple in our church offered to care for Keith
until we could manage him ourselves. I couldn't believe

**Patti learned
the value
of kindness
from her
Michigan
hometown;
Patti (left),
Mom and
sister Debbie.**

they were willing to take on a newborn when
they had two young boys at home. Their help
made all the difference.

We benefited from many other acts of kindness.
The local Catholic church held a Mass for Mom—
and we weren't Catholic! Meals showed up at
dinnertime for weeks. The lawn got mowed, and
I don't think Dad even knew who was doing it.

Keith stayed with his surrogate family for over
a month—and the story ends happily. He grew
like little babies do, Mom recovered, and I grew
up a little faster than planned, but oh, so grateful.

Years later, my friend Helen found out she was going
to have twins, and her little girl would be 15 months
old when the babies arrived. Not only did we hold a
baby shower, but I organized the effort to have dinner
delivered for the first few weeks she was home.

Helen, who grew up in a suburb in California, had
never heard of such a thing—people going out of their
way to help someone else. She was used to not even
knowing her neighbors. But I said, "We're transplanted
Midwesterners, and we take care of our own!" ☀

Angels in the Gristmill

Helping those in need is the right thing to do.

BY DOUGLAS SCOTT CLARK
Maryville, Tennessee

My father asked if I would go with him to his family's old homeplace. Dad wanted to see if his father's old mill was still standing.

When we arrived, he paused to gently touch the hand-hewn logs and then we entered the old musty building. "It was my job to gauge how much corn fell into the millstones," Dad said, showing me where he'd stood. "More corn meant coarser meal."

We stared into the hopper for a moment before he added, "When poor folks brought their nubbin corn to be ground into meal, Poppa and me kind of helped them. I took a little good corn from Poppa's toll box and mixed it with theirs. Their corn was barely fit for feeding chickens."

"And you and Grandpa never told anyone?" I asked.

"Nary a soul. If we had, folks would be beholden to us. That just didn't set right with country folks. You don't go tooting your own horn."

I'll never forget how Grandpa and Dad helped their neighbors without expecting a single thing in return. To me, they were true angels. ☀

A young Amish couple ride past Compton's Mill here in Somerset County.
CAROL SAYLOR *Meyersdale, Pennsylvania*

A Stone's Throw

Sharing magic makes all the difference.

BY DAVID WARREN *Kettering, Ohio*

I had to be coaxed into the hike. My wife, who puts hiking in the fall at the top of her list of favorite things to do, reminded me how we had hiked when we were first dating. I moaned and groaned about wanting to watch football instead, but as the sun glistened atop the leaves I was swayed to join her.

As our hike progressed, I had to admit that the fresh fall air and unexpected warmth made the time in the woods rather enjoyable. I glanced over at some kids playing near a stream. One of them exclaimed that he had found some shells. My wife loves shells, so she jumped up and walked over to see for herself. Sure enough, the kids were right. There were shells in this southern Ohio stream. She grabbed one and held it up like a prize.

I began to look around for shells also, and although I saw a few, what really caught my eye was a perfectly flat stone on the ground. I eagerly reached to pick it up. In an instant I recalled skipping stones as a kid. Watching a flat stone skip across the top of the water seven or eight times was like watching some sort of magic trick.

I told my wife she could keep her shells; I had found some skipping stones. She gave me a puzzled look and asked, "What are skipping stones?" I showed my find to her and told her to watch me as I flung the stone so that it hit the water and then skipped along the surface several times.

She looked on in amazement and asked, "How do you do that?" I gave her a quick lesson. After just a few attempts, she was a pro.

For a couple of perfect minutes I stood behind my wife and wrapped my arms around her waist. I could tell she was content and proud of her new skill. I was glad I was there to share in it. We had so much fun, we hadn't noticed the sun fading behind the trees.

As a boy I thought skipping a stone was something magical. As a middle-aged man, sharing this moment with the woman I have loved for more than 20 years was beyond magical. That's the beauty of life. The simple and unexpected moments are almost always the best ones. ☀

Simple treasures abound in nature.

Lucky Little Oliver

A few inches saved a beloved family tractor from a devastating tornado.

BY JOY BALLY GRADERT *Cambridge, Illinois*

In 1943, when our Oliver 70 tractor first rolled off the assembly line, there was no telling what kind of life it would end up leading. My grandfather Emil Ebinger was renting a 120-acre grain and livestock farm near Washington, Illinois, and he used that Oliver 70 to raise all of his corn, oats and hay.

By 1957, my grandfather had saved enough money to purchase a farm in Dahlgren, Illinois. He trucked the Oliver south to Wayne County, where he used it to grind cattle feed, spray fencerows and haul baled hay. In the fall, it sported a two-row mounted picker.

My grandfather's health deteriorated, and he reluctantly scheduled a machinery auction in 1970. The Oliver was listed on the sale bill, but when sale day came, my grandfather couldn't bear to part with it. After the sale, he handed the keys to his grandson, my brother, Randall Bally.

Randy hauled the Oliver back north to his grain farm in Woodford County, where it was a chore tractor. Several years later, Randy parked it between two grain trucks in his old converted livestock barn. It sat there quietly, almost forgotten, until Nov. 17, 2013.

Joy's son restored the '43 Oliver 70 (top). Inset shows the tractor before renovation.

On that Sunday, much of Washington, Illinois, blew away in an EF4 tornado. The funnel cloud continued northeast across rural Woodford County, in a direct path to Randy's farm.

After the tornado, the old livestock barn was lying in a big heap, but amazingly, most of the farm machinery was still sitting where Randy had parked it. The huge barn rafters had come down directly on the two trucks parked on either side of the Oliver. They missed the tractor's fenders and hood by inches; only its exhaust pipe was damaged by falling debris. The tractor sure was lucky.

During cleanup, my brother decided to give the little Oliver to his nephew—my son, Keith—who tore apart the engine, ground the valves and replaced the rings. He found a new seat and new rear tires, and then he had the tractor professionally painted.

The Oliver won't be asked to work anymore. And if things go as planned, ownership will someday be transferred to Keith's nephew, Gregory, Emil's great-great-grandson—the fifth generation to own the lucky little Oliver. ☀

Barn Full of Blessings

Love and laughter replace cows and equipment on this family farm.

BY WHITNEY MILLER *Franklin, Tennessee*

Merriam-Webster defines a barn as "a usually large building for the storage of farm products or feed and usually for the housing of farm animals or farm equipment."

Such was the case for my great-grandparents' barn in Lumberton, Mississippi, which is now long gone. But my family's modern-day barn—built in the shadow of the original—takes the "usually" part of the definition to heart. Usually, but not always. Sometimes a barn houses love.

Whitney Miller (standing) dreamed of getting married in a barn. Her father, John Miller (in blue), built one perfect for both weddings and holiday gatherings.

A paper table runner is transformed into a doodle station with seasonal rubber stamps. For a rustic buffet, the family created a quick table from whiskey barrels and an old board.

With the help of a friend, my dad began building a small barn for his farm equipment three years ago. At the time, my sister and I had both become engaged, and we dreamed of weddings in a big barn with weathered wood and chandeliers. So Dad changed his plans. His small barn became a big one, and it doesn't house his farm equipment. That fall, on a beautiful Thanksgiving weekend, my husband and I said "I do" in Dad's new barn. We celebrated alongside friends and family with food, music and dancing.

Today, our barn continues to be a gathering place for not only special occasions, but also for Sunday dinners and holiday meals. Having a large space for everyone to gather together on Thanksgiving is important to big families like mine. Each family member arrives with food in hand—Nanny Ida with her famous rolls, my mom with her traditional cornbread dressing and my sister, Brittyn, with coconut cream pie. There are Dad's deviled eggs and my carrot souffle. It is a smorgasbord of family favorites.

Rustic tables line the barn floor, covered with simple table runners made from painter's drop cloths. We reflect on the words of the traditional children's prayer, Let Us Thank Him, on the runners. My sister adds a white dough bowl filled with green succulents and pumpkins for a centerpiece.

Once everyone finds a place, we take the time to share what we are thankful for. Being grateful is truly a theme for my family during this time of year. We remember those who are not with us and celebrate new lives in the family—my baby son among them. The kids then say the Lord's Prayer, and Dad follows with his blessing over the meal.

With that, it's time to eat! In our barn, the line to fill our plates always forms from the oldest to the youngest. With clear glass plates full of delicious food, we slip our silverware from handmade brown paper sleeves and begin enjoying our meals. Silence fills the barn for just a moment—until someone says, "Pass the rolls, please." ☀

DOG TAG: BRAT82/SHUTTERSTOCK

Brothers in Arms

Each son left the farm to serve his country on the battlefield,
and each left something behind.

BY JIM COBURN *Selma, Alabama*

In 1941, the oldest of five brothers took off his old blue denim work shirt. He hung it on a nail driven into the bedroom door of the farmhouse where he lived with his family.

On that same day, he went into the service. Later that year, the United States entered World War II.

In 1942, the second oldest brother took a nail and drove it into the bedroom door beside the blue denim shirt. He took off his work shirt and hung it there. On that day, he, too, went into service.

A year later, the third oldest brother drove a nail into the bedroom door and hung his own work shirt. On that day, he went into the service.

In 1944, the oldest brother was reported missing in action. In 1945, he was declared dead.

Young brothers Paul, Jim, Tom, Quentin and Fred (from left) play on the farm tractor.

At the end of the war, the second-oldest brother came home and reclaimed his work shirt. In 1946, the third-oldest brother did the same. Only the oldest brother's shirt remained.

In 1950, another war. Another brother. Another blue denim work shirt.

In 1951, the fifth and youngest brother took off his work shirt and hung it opposite the oldest one. On that day, he went into service.

The fourth and fifth brothers returned home and reclaimed their work shirts. But the oldest blue denim shirt still hung there, undisturbed.

It's been years since I've been to the old house. I hear it is weathered and falling down. I think of it often, and when I do, I wonder if the oldest brother's work shirt is there. And this, my friends, is a true story—for one of those shirts was mine. ☀

Roasted Green Vegetable Medley

PREP: 20 min. • **BAKE:** 20 min.
MAKES: 10 servings

1	lb. fresh green beans, trimmed and cut into 2-in. pieces
4	cups fresh broccoli florets
10	small fresh mushrooms, halved
8	fresh Brussels sprouts, halved
2	medium carrots, cut into ¼-in. slices
1	medium onion, halved and sliced
3 to 5	garlic cloves, thinly sliced
4	Tbsp. olive oil, divided
½	cup grated Parmesan cheese
3	Tbsp. julienned fresh basil leaves, optional
2	Tbsp. minced fresh parsley
1	Tbsp. grated lemon peel
2	Tbsp. lemon juice
¼	tsp. salt
¼	tsp. pepper

1. Preheat oven to 425°. Place first seven ingredients in a large bowl; toss with 2 Tbsp. oil. Divide between two 15x10x1-in. pans coated with cooking spray.
2. Roast until tender, 20-25 minutes, stirring occasionally. Transfer to a large bowl. Mix remaining ingredients with remaining oil; toss with vegetables.

1 serving: 109 cal., 7g fat (1g sat. fat), 3mg chol., 96mg sod., 10g carb. (3g sugars, 3g fiber), 4g pro.
Diabetic exchanges: 1 vegetable, 1 fat.

Spiced Ambrosia Punch

PREP: 15 min. • **COOK:** 3 hours
MAKES: 10 servings

- 3½ cups apple cider or juice
- 3 cups apricot nectar
- 1 cup peach nectar or additional apricot nectar
- ¼ cup water
- 3 Tbsp. lemon juice
- ½ tsp. ground cardamom
- ½ tsp. ground nutmeg
- 2 cinnamon sticks (3 in.)
- 1 tsp. finely chopped fresh gingerroot
- 1 tsp. grated orange zest
- 8 whole cloves
  Orange slices and lemon peel strips, optional

1. In a 3- or 4-qt. slow cooker, combine first seven ingredients. Place cinnamon sticks, ginger, orange zest and cloves on a double thickness of cheesecloth. Gather corners of cloth to enclose seasonings; tie securely with string. Add to slow cooker.
2. Cook, covered, on low until flavors are blended, 3-4 hours. Discard spice bag. Serve warm. If desired, garnish with orange slices and lemon peel.

¾ cup: 115 cal., 0 fat (0 sat. fat), 0 chol., 14mg sod., 29g carb. (26g sugars, 1g fiber), 0 pro.

Slow-Cooker Sauerbraten

PREP: 20 min. • **COOK:** 6 hours • **MAKES:** 8 servings

- 1 bottle (14 oz.) ketchup
- 1 large onion, chopped
- ¾ cup packed brown sugar
- ¾ cup cider vinegar
- 1 Tbsp. mixed pickling spices
- 3 bay leaves
- 1 boneless beef chuck roast or rump roast (3 to 4 lbs.)
- 4 cups water
- 1½ cups crushed gingersnap cookies (about 30 cookies)
- 2 Tbsp. cornstarch
- ¼ cup cold water

1. Mix first six ingredients. Place roast in a 5-qt. slow cooker; add water. Pour ketchup mixture over top. Add cookie crumbs. Cook, covered, on low until meat is tender, 6-8 hours.
2. Remove roast from slow cooker; keep warm. Strain cooking juices; skim fat. Transfer 4 cups juices to a saucepan; bring to a boil. Mix the cornstarch and water until smooth; stir into cooking juices. Return to a boil; cook and stir until thickened, 1-2 minutes. Serve with roast.

1 serving: 475 cal., 11g fat (3g sat. fat), 101mg chol., 858mg sod., 58g carb. (40g sugars, 1g fiber), 35g pro.

Sweet Potato & Carrot Casserole

PREP: 55 min. • **BAKE:** 25 min. + standing
MAKES: 12 servings

½	cup golden raisins
3½	lbs. medium sweet potatoes (about 6 potatoes)
4	large carrots, cut into 1½-in. pieces
¼	cup butter
1½	cups packed brown sugar
⅓	cup orange juice

1. Preheat oven to 375°. In a small bowl, cover raisins with hot water; let stand 30 minutes.
2. Place potatoes in a 6-qt. stockpot; add water to cover. Bring to a boil. Reduce heat; cook, uncovered, just until tender, 15-20 minutes. Remove potatoes and cool slightly. Add carrots to same pot of boiling water; cook, uncovered, until tender, 15-20 minutes; drain.
3. Peel sweet potatoes and cut crosswise into 1½-in.-thick slices. Arrange potatoes and carrots in a greased 13x9-in. baking dish, cut sides down.
4. Drain raisins. In a small saucepan, melt butter over medium heat; stir in raisins. Add brown sugar and orange juice, stirring to dissolve sugar. Pour over vegetables.
5. Bake, uncovered, until mixture is heated through and sauce is bubbly, 25-30 minutes; if desired, baste occasionally with sauce. Let stand 10 minutes; toss before serving.

¾ cup: 307 cal., 4g fat (2g sat. fat), 10mg chol., 69mg sod., 67g carb. (45g sugars, 5g fiber), 3g pro.

Creamy Cranberry Salad

PREP: 15 min. + chilling • **MAKES:** 16 servings

3	cups fresh or thawed frozen cranberries, chopped
1	can (20 oz.) unsweetened crushed pineapple, drained
2	cups miniature marshmallows
1	medium apple, chopped
⅔	cup sugar
⅛	tsp. salt
2	cups heavy whipping cream
¼	cup chopped walnuts

1. In a large bowl, mix first six ingredients. Refrigerate, covered, overnight.
2. To serve, beat cream until stiff peaks form. Fold whipped cream and walnuts into cranberry mixture.

½ cup: 200 cal., 12g fat (7g sat. fat), 34mg chol., 32mg sod., 23g carb. (20g sugars, 1g fiber), 1g pro.

Make-Ahead Turkey & Gravy

PREP: 4¼ hours + freezing · **BAKE:** 50 min.
MAKES: 16 servings (2½ cups gravy)

- 1 **turkey (14 to 16 lbs.)**
- 2 **tsp. poultry seasoning**
- 1 **tsp. pepper**
- 3 **cups chicken broth**
- ½ **cup minced fresh parsley**
- 1 **Tbsp. minced fresh thyme or 1 tsp. dried thyme**
- 1 **Tbsp. minced fresh rosemary or 1 tsp. dried rosemary, crushed**
- 2 **tsp. grated lemon zest**
- ¼ **cup lemon juice**
- 2 **garlic cloves, minced**

FOR SERVING
- 1½ **cups chicken broth**
- 1 **Tbsp. butter**
- 1 **Tbsp. all-purpose flour**

1. Preheat oven to 325°. Place turkey on a rack in a roasting pan, breast side up. Sprinkle with poultry seasoning and pepper. Tuck wings under turkey; tie drumsticks together.

2. Roast, uncovered, 30 minutes. In a 4-cup measuring cup, mix broth, herbs, lemon zest and juice, and garlic; pour over turkey. Roast, uncovered, until a thermometer inserted in thickest part of thigh reads 170°-175°, 3-3½ hours, basting occasionally with broth mixture. Cover loosely with foil if turkey browns too quickly.

3. Remove turkey from pan; let stand at least 20 minutes before carving. Skim fat from cooking juices.

To freeze: Carve turkey and place in shallow freezer containers. Pour cooking juices over turkey; cool slightly, about 1 hour. Cover and freeze up to 3 months.

To serve: Partially thaw turkey in refrigerator overnight. Preheat oven to 350°. Transfer turkey and cooking juices to a large baking dish. Pour 1½ cups broth over top. Bake, covered, until a thermometer inserted in turkey reads 165°, 50-60 minutes.

To prepare gravy: Remove turkey to a platter, reserving broth mixture; keep warm. In a saucepan, melt butter over medium heat; stir in flour until smooth. Gradually whisk in broth mixture; bring to a boil, stirring constantly. Cook and stir until thickened, about 2 minutes. Serve with turkey.

8 oz. cooked turkey with about 2½ Tbsp. gravy: 480 cal., 22g fat (7g sat. fat), 218mg chol., 434mg sod., 2g carb. (1g sugars, 0 fiber), 64g pro.

Caramel-Pecan Apple Pie

PREP: 45 min.
BAKE: 65 min. + cooling
MAKES: 8 servings

Pastry for single-crust pie (9 in.)
- 7 cups sliced peeled tart apples (about 6 medium)
- 1 tsp. lemon juice
- 1 tsp. vanilla extract
- ¾ cup chopped pecans
- ⅓ cup packed brown sugar
- 3 Tbsp. sugar
- 4 tsp. ground cinnamon
- 1 Tbsp. cornstarch
- ¼ cup caramel topping, room temperature
- 3 Tbsp. butter, melted

STREUSEL TOPPING
- ¾ cup all-purpose flour
- ¼ cup sugar
- 6 Tbsp. cold butter, cubed
- ⅔ cup chopped pecans
- ¼ cup caramel topping, room temperature

Whipped cream and additional caramel topping, optional

1. Preheat oven to 350°. On a lightly floured surface, roll crust to a ⅛-in.-thick circle; transfer to a 9-in. deep-dish pie plate. Trim crust to ½ in. beyond rim of plate; flute edge. Refrigerate until ready to fill.
2. In a large bowl, toss apples with lemon juice and vanilla. Mix pecans, sugars, cinnamon and cornstarch; add to apples and toss to combine.
3. Spread caramel topping onto bottom of crust. Fill with apple mixture. Drizzle with butter.
4. For streusel topping, mix flour and sugar. Cut in butter until crumbly; stir in pecans. Sprinkle over filling.
5. Bake on a lower oven rack until filling is bubbly, 65-75 minutes. Drizzle with caramel topping. Cool on a wire rack. If desired, serve with whipped cream and additional caramel topping.

1 piece: 639 cal., 39g fat (17g sat. fat), 64mg chol., 331mg sod., 73g carb. (43g sugars, 5g fiber), 6g pro.

Sausage Dressing

PREP: 20 min. • **COOK:** 3 hours • **MAKES:** 10 servings

- 1 **lb. bulk pork sausage**
- 1 **large onion, chopped**
- 2 **celery ribs, chopped**
- 1 **can (14½ oz.) chicken broth**
- 2 **large eggs, lightly beaten**
- ¼ **cup butter, melted**
- 1½ **tsp. rubbed sage**
- ½ **tsp. pepper**
- 1 **pkg. (14 oz.) seasoned stuffing cubes (about 9 cups)**
- 1 **large tart apple, chopped**
- 1 **cup chopped walnuts or pecans**

1. In a large skillet, cook and crumble sausage with onion and celery over medium heat until no longer pink, 5-7 minutes. Using a slotted spoon, transfer sausage mixture to a greased 5-qt. slow cooker.
2. Stir in broth, eggs, melted butter, sage and pepper. Add remaining ingredients; mix lightly to combine.
3. Cook, covered, on low until a thermometer inserted in center reads 165°, 3-4 hours, stirring once.

⅔ **cup:** 412 cal., 25g fat (7g sat. fat), 75mg chol., 1080mg sod., 37g carb. (5g sugars, 4g fiber), 13g pro.

Beef Roast Dinner

PREP: 25 min. • **COOK:** 7 hours • **MAKES:** 8 servings

- 1 **lb. red potatoes (3-4 medium), cubed**
- 1½ **cups fresh baby carrots**
- 1 **medium green pepper, chopped**
- 1 **medium parsnip, chopped**
- ¼ **lb. small fresh mushrooms**
- 1 **small red onion, chopped**
- 1 **beef rump roast or bottom round roast (3 lbs.)**
- 1 **can (14½ oz.) beef broth**
- ¾ **tsp. salt**
- ¾ **tsp. dried oregano**
- ¼ **tsp. pepper**
- 3 **Tbsp. cornstarch**
- ¼ **cup cold water**

1. Place vegetables in a 5-qt. slow cooker. Cut roast in half; place over vegetables. Mix broth and seasonings; pour over roast. Cook, covered, on low until meat and vegetables are tender, 7-9 hours.
2. Remove roast and vegetables from slow cooker; keep warm. Transfer cooking juices to a small saucepan; bring to a boil. Mix cornstarch and water until smooth; stir into cooking juices. Return to a boil; cook and stir until thickened, 1-2 minutes. Serve with roast and vegetables.

1 serving: 304 cal., 8g fat (3g sat. fat), 101mg chol., 533mg sod., 19g carb. (4g sugars, 3g fiber), 36g pro.
Diabetic exchanges: 5 lean meat, 1 starch.

HANDCRAFTED WITH LOVE

Creepy Cottage

This miniature scene is big on frightful fun.

WHAT YOU'LL NEED

- Ceramic house
- Black matte spray paint
- Acrylic paints
- Hollow carvable foam pumpkin
- Battery-operated mini LED light string
- Fairy garden bench
- Spice jar lids, optional
- Moss
- Paintbrushes
- Drill
- Hot glue gun

DIRECTIONS

1. Spray-paint ceramic house. Dry thoroughly. Paint house details with acrylic paints, if desired. Paint pumpkin interior with acrylic paint. Dry thoroughly. Add any additional details.
2. Using ¼-in. drill bit, drill a hole in the back of the pumpkin near the bottom. Insert light string through hole and spread lights on the floor.
3. Arrange the house and bench inside pumpkin. Hot-glue to the floor, using jar lids underneath to add height if needed. Glue moss to floor and around the jar lids.

Hoot Halloween

No need for messy carving with these wise old owls dressed in vintage newsprint feathers.

WHAT YOU'LL NEED
- Scrapbook paper in assorted colors
- Color copies of yellowed book pages and newspaper
- Scrapbook scissors with specialty edges
- Scissors
- Scalloped circle punch
- Double-stick tape
- Straight pins
- White pumpkins

DIRECTIONS
1. Sketch a design on paper for the owl's face and wings. Using regular and specialty scissors and a circle punch, cut designs from scrapbook paper and photocopied pages. Consider cutting multiple layers for each element, layering them for the desired effect. Cut fringe on the edges of top layer of wings for feathers, if desired.
2. Layer designs using small pieces of double-stick tape.
3. Secure pieces to pumpkins with straight pins. If desired, use pins with decorative heads for additional embellishment.

Can Boo!

Light the night with spooktacular luminaries.

WHAT YOU'LL NEED
- 3 clean tin cans
- Black spray paint made for metal
- Orange grease marker
- 1 spring clamp
- Drill with metal drill bit or a nail, a block of wood and a hammer
- Orange tissue paper
- Black tape
- Small battery-operated candles

DIRECTIONS
1. Coat insides and outsides of the cans with spray paint. Use several sheer coats of paint for even coverage.
2. With the grease marker, make dots that form one letter of the word "BOO" on each can. Placing the dots in the valleys of the cans' ridges makes drilling or hammering easier.
3. Clamp the can to a table; use the drill (or a hammer and a nail with a block of wood inside the can) to punch holes.
4. Cut squares of tissue paper that are ½ in. larger than the punched letters, and tape them inside the can behind the pierced holes of each letter.
5. Illuminate cans using battery-operated candles.

Winter

Snow lies like whipped frosting on the
ground and on tree limbs near this bridge
in Northfield Falls, Vermont.
PHOTO BY JOHN H. KNOX

THE GOOD LIFE

Winters on the Wabash

Ice and snow transform an Indiana river into a frozen playground.

BY RAYMOND L. SNOKE *Lebanon, Indiana*

Grandpa Snoke had just come indoors from feeding his many cats and Poncho, his miniature beagle. Outside it was near zero, and a few inches of snow covered the ground, giving the land the look of an absolute winter wonderland.

Grandma was in the kitchen cooking a pan of cornmeal mush with fresh sausage crumbled into thesizzling slices. Along with a bowl of steaming hot oatmeal covered in brown sugar and cream, this was a breakfast fit for a king. As usual, I also grabbed a couple of freshly baked cookies from the cookie jar to dunk into my cereal.

Having eaten until my tummy was as full as a tick's, I ventured out onto the frozen tundra of the Wabash River Valley. As I left the warm confines of my grandparents' home, which was 10 miles outside of Logansport, Indiana, the cold hit me. Icy air attempted to invade my body by any means it could. No matter how tightly I bundled up, the frigid air eventually found its way to my supposedly covered flesh. It was so brutally cold that Poncho didn't even come out of his doghouse to greet me.

On this day, the creek that ran through their property was higher than normal. Water spilled over the rock dams that Grandpa had built, and unusual ice formations were being created as the cold creek water neared the icy Wabash.

In one spot, a small ice cavern was forming as water running over the rocks gradually froze in layers. During the summer months I would play and splash in the water. But this time of year, I wanted to do just about anything except get wet.

As I stood shivering along the bank, I saw pieces of ice the size of a house drifting down the river, which was clearer than normal. Toward January, much of the water would ordinarily be frozen, except for faster flowing

In the Wabash River Valley, water is a big part of childhood.

channels on the south side of the Wabash. Though the ice seemed thick enough along the bank, I dared not venture out onto it for fear that I might fall through and not be found until the spring thaw.

Across the road from my grandparents' was a small prairie with a creek bed etching its way back and forth across it. The creek's water was shallow and its bottom made of solid limestone. This portion once fed into an operating gristmill under their cabin. Although the large metal wheel no longer turns, it is still there, inviting the curious passerby to see just how well things made long ago can stand the test of time.

Off toward the north, a larger creek (name unknown to me) fed a smaller stream that ran toward the mill. When I went there I could almost feel the presence of those pioneers as they made a living from a hostile and foreign land. Their survival depended totally on their ability to turn the harsh landscape into productive farms, to hunt, to fish and to build solid and secure homes for their families. Of course these daring ancestors also relied on their faith in God, who made all of it possible.

As my stomach began to yearn for one of Grandma's lunches, I slowly turned back toward their homeplace, where I found warmth, security and love. ☀

Mills like this one in Parke County, Indiana, were a staple of rural America.

Welcome to Snow Town

Every winter day takes my breath away in Alaska's snow capital, 250 miles from the nearest stoplight.

BY CINDY BUTHERUS *Valdez, Alaska*

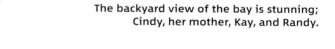

The backyard view of the bay is stunning;
Cindy, her mother, Kay, and Randy.

Valdez, Alaska, known as Snow Town, gets more snow than any other area in the state. On average, 300 inches fall in town each year, and 600 inches fall in Thompson Pass coming into town. Valdez is in a sheltered bay of Prince William Sound, surrounded by the mighty Chugach Mountains. The nearest stoplight is over 250 miles away in Palmer.

My husband, Randy, and I live on the edge of Valdez. Our street was part of a homestead long before a bridge crossed Mineral Creek to get to the area. The owners barged their supplies to the beach and then hauled them

home. When they sold the homestead, they gave the majority of the property to the state to be preserved.

We look upon mountains from every window, with waterfalls coming off the mountain across the street from the front and east end of our house, and bay views out the back when foliage and snow allow. We can see an eagle's nest when the leaves are gone. We admire lovely, untouched nature that changes with the seasons to the point that it seems we live in two different places without having to move.

Randy's sister Sheri, who is our neighbor, moved here in the late 1980s from western Washington. We fell in

Even those who don't like snow admit that this is one of the most beautiful settings they've ever seen.

love with the area on our first visit here in 1989, despite the chaos after the oil spill. It took us 10 years to move, finally arriving in September 1999.

I have been employed with the local electric co-op since 2001, and Randy has worked for Alaska Department of Transportation as a parts manager for the equipment fleet since 2006. Randy helps to maintain the snowplows and the graders that keep Thompson Pass open and drivable year round.

We get plenty of moisture from the coast, and the mountains keep extreme interior cold out, so we stay in the perfect snow zone—teens and 20s for the most part. This makes for some great shots of our dog, Ruffy, playing in the weather that he loves so much. Ruffy likes to roll in the snow, help Randy dig the snow out, and play Frisbee or ball.

We have the best snow removal in the world, so weather doesn't stop anybody from getting to work or school. Valdez was relocated after a 1964 earthquake, and the Army Corps of Engineers laid out the new town, including drainage and snow storage requirements.

There are snow lots, so the plows don't have to push the snow far. That helps, as we can get many feet of snow in a day. Without the drainage system, we'd flood every spring, but the city keeps the drains clear.

Ruffy, the family dog, leaps for a Frisbee; snowfalls in Valdez are often measured in feet, not inches.

Getting out of (or back into) our one-story house after the roof has shed a big accumulation requires some work. Randy likes to call it his "snowercise." But after a heavy storm, the sun comes out, and it is so stunning, quiet and peaceful.

In early winter, we have about five hours of daylight, and the sun doesn't completely rise above the mountain peaks across the bay, causing a peekaboo effect. But by the end of January the sun has risen high enough to clear the mountains again.

In late winter, avalanches start coming off the mountains. They are something quite powerful to watch.

Pictures can't do full justice to nature's gift of beauty. With the mountains so close and so breathtaking, tourists stop in the middle of the road to stare!

It's true that a full-time life in Valdez is not for everyone. With its extreme climate, people either love it or hate it. But even those who don't like snow admit that this is one of the most beautiful settings they've ever seen. I still am in awe myself after all these years. ☀

The Long-Lost Cabin

*Recovering our family's ancestral home
brought the past into the present.*

BY JUNE CHILDS *Dresden, Tennessee*

Come with me to a log cabin that sits back in the yard and draws the attention of many who drive along our lovely country road in Tennessee.

My great-grandfather Henry C. Carney, whose portrait hangs over the fireplace, built the one-room structure in the 1840s and raised his family here. William, his son and my grandfather, did the same.

At some point, a country home was built around the cabin, hiding it from view. The property was sold, and lost to our family until the day we bought it back.

The neighbor who owned the country home was tearing it down. My husband, Brad, had heard the story of the hidden cabin and went over to see for himself. There it was,

right in the middle of what used to be the newer home. Brad told the neighbor that this was my ancestral home and offered to buy it. The neighbor was so kind. Though he'd wanted the cabin for himself, he sold it to us for a very reasonable price.

Moving the cabin wasn't easy. Two wonderful neighbors put it on logs and pulled it with a tractor to our yard.

Once we had the cabin on our property, the real work began. We made discoveries that connected us to the past. For example, at the time the cabin was built, my great-grandfather carved his and his wife's names into the logs on the side of the building. These carvings were still visible in the wood. We learned that the beams were cut from trees found in the area and processed at the sawmill.

June Childs and her husband, Brad (seated), are surrounded by family on the newly built porch of the old Carney cabin.

I am grateful for each home and all the generations of family they represent. I feel blessed to be surrounded by this heritage.

With the help of family and friends, we restored the cabin. We chinked the logs with concrete and added a new porch, a roof, a half loft and windows. To support the new front porch, we used original sandstone from our old stock barn, which was destroyed by a tornado after Thanksgiving in 1994.

Another neighbor made new doors by hand, each complete with the type of wooden hinges and drop handles that would likely have been on the original doors.

Once the structure was sound, I filled it with keepsakes from my childhood, including a school desk, my grandmother's sewing machine and a recitation bench. We placed a bed in the loft and draped a quilt that my mother made across it. A washstand is beside the bed.

The cabin is now a gathering place, where we have had many festive meals seated at the very table where I ate as a child.

Outside, looking across my large yard, I see three memorable family homes. The first is the one my parents built in 1923 (our daughter raised her children in that house and now my grandson lives there). That's where I grew up, and I treasure every day of my happy childhood. Brad and I built the second one more than 40 years ago. We raised our girls there. The Carney cabin is the third.

I am grateful for each home and all the generations of family they represent. I feel blessed to be surrounded by this heritage. ☀

Feeling Like a Kid Again

Big, beautiful snowflakes bring grown-ups out to play.

BY JUDY WRODA *Ashville, New York*

I woke up this morning, crawled out from under the heavy, warm comforter, and went directly to the kitchen to make a pot of coffee. Then I shuffled into the living room, put some wood on the fire and opened the drapes to see what the morning had brought me. The sight of massive snowflakes took my breath away. I smiled wide, and my heart skipped happily in anticipation of a gorgeous winter day.

Bundled up in warm clothes, wool socks, a heavy coat, mittens and a scarf, I went outside. The dog followed me. I had to lift my feet high and take small steps due to the depth of the snow. Quite deep, quite beautiful, somewhat wet. I made the first snowball, picked it up and patted it tight. Good, firm, just right. I rolled that snowball until it was too heavy to roll.

I was on my knees pushing it for the last few turns. I parked that huge snowball right by the front porch, then I went back to build another, smaller one.

I made the second snowball and had to get my friend Bob to help hoist it onto the first one. Then I went back to make a third. My fingers and cheeks were frozen, but my heart was warm and laughter came freely, echoing in the valley. I picked up the third snowball and heaved it up on top.

For the finishing touches, I found two branches just crying out to be arms, so arms they became. Next I walked over to the evergreen to pluck some small red and green ornaments for buttons and eyes. Then I went into the cabin, to the refrigerator, and found some more treasures to add.

When I was done, I stood back to admire my handiwork. Not bad for an old lady! The snowman was close to 6 feet tall, with red ornament buttons on his tummy and a carrot for his nose. He had two small green ornaments for eyes and three smaller carrots arranged into a smile. A bright scarf circled his nonexistent neck, and a cowboy hat, held on by a thick icicle, graced his head.

The snow was still falling, only the flakes were a bit bigger. The dog watched me, bewildered by my childlike enthusiasm. Today, I played in the snow. ☀

Judy frolicked in the snow on this glorious winter morning.

Sheldon the Too-Short Christmas Tree

This fir gave the phrase "cut to size" a whole new meaning.

BY KRISTA OTTINGER *Colfax, Wisconsin*

There is a tree in my living room. Well, there is a portion of a tree in my living room.

We tried a new tree farm the other day. Well, actually we tried an old tree farm the other day.

We were fed up with paying $40 for a Christmas tree, so this year we decided to check out the $10 trees south of town. The sign said, "Cut Your Own Tree to Size for $10." You plop your money into the slot and head out to the back forty, armed with one of the farm's shiny bow saws. You fell whichever of the 30- to 40-foot trees looks best, then you lop off the top and thread that onto your vehicle. Nothing fancy.

At eye level, the upper portion of our Fraser fir—or maybe it was a Canaan or a Douglas; there were no signs or sections in the field of trees, so we weren't sure—looked slightly different than it did when we'd seen it upright, but we did a pretty good job. I was afraid when we brought it down it would be a lot bigger than we thought, but the opposite was the case. This was one skinny tree.

When we picked it out, we were eager to see all the cones adorning the branches at the top, but up close, we saw we'd chosen a tree that harbored a plethora of now

Krista and her husband cut their own tree using bow saws, just like the folks pictured above.

tiny cone-skeletons. The squirrels had eaten well this fall.

Nevertheless, we brought the top 10 feet home to cram into a tree stand that has never housed anything less than a monster. We name our trees, and they often earn monikers like Hagrid for their ceiling-scraping immensity. Sheldon, as this one is known, sits meekly in his stand, looking like a toddler in Dad's hunting boots. The breeze I kick up walking by jostles Shel around like a windstorm.

Poor Sheldon is getting a bad rap, but I'll take the blame for most of that. When we got him home, as my husband and I parted ways at the van—he to measure and cut Sheldon to size and I to clear the patch of real estate the tree would occupy in the living room—it was I who said, "Cut him to 7 feet. The ceiling is a little more than that, but the stand will raise him up. Seven should be perfect."

It was not perfect. Our ceiling is not 7 feet high. I doubt yours is. I don't know what I was thinking. So now, our awkward Sheldon is vertically challenged. His angel is staring skyward, wondering why the ceiling is so far away. But good news: Sheldon offers easy watering and gift placement. ☀

SCRAPBOOK

As the bright evening sun began to drop, these horses added
a touch of grace to this snowy scene. What a peaceful day!
LYLE EBERLE *Olds, Alberta*

In Yosemite National Park, the clouds moved in quickly as if to give
the El Capitan rock formation a big hug—like saying hello to an old friend.
ROBBIN CHERRY *San Jose, California*

For some winter fun on our family ranch, Dad pulled the boys through the deep snow while I followed behind with our dogs in case one of the kiddos fell overboard.
TRISHA GOETTLE *Avon, Montana*

I feed the deer around my home and continually take photos and videos of them.
On this day, I was lucky to capture their festive winter frolicking.
TRUDY WHEELER *Havelock, Ontario*

I waited all winter for this noble varied thrush
to come close enough for a portrait.
SALLY HARRIS *Carlsborg, Washington*

My granddaughter Cardin loves Pudding,
an Australorp-Black Maran hen.
JOHN DAVIDSON *Upland, California*

My brother, Joshua, wanted to stay outside with these gentle giants despite the cold.
McKENNA SONNETT *Billings, Montana*

Our daughter Cora wanted a puppy for Christmas. It was love at first sight!
SARAH ROGERS *Coxs Creek, Kentucky*

I love to take pictures of birds that visit my feeder. Northern cardinals are some of my favorites.
ELSIE JONES *Allegan, Michigan*

The hay rake was still hooked to the tractor during our first snowfall. The scene was so beautiful, and I couldn't resist taking a picture.
JANET MORETZ *Boone, North Carolina*

A snow-covered drive leads the
way to a New England farm
filled with Christmas cheer.
PHOTO BY PAUL REZENDES

These boys of mine bring me so much joy. Pictured (from left) are McCoy, Jake the miniature pony and Merritt. The adorable cowboys sure look ready for a ride.
HAYLEY MOSS *Hull, Iowa*

There's nothing better than a pet hen who enjoys everything you let her try, like riding a toboggan.
ERIN LANGSDORF *Eugene, Oregon*

My wife, Christie, and I live close to Rocky Mountain National Park and often
spend Sundays on Trail Ridge Road, which soars to 12,183 feet above sea level.
BRUCE SHAVER *Longmont, Colorado*

Yosemite Valley Chapel looked so inspirational and peaceful as snow fell one Sunday morning in Yosemite National Park.
SHARON McWHIRTER *Citrus Heights, California*

As snowflakes fly, this mom and daughter take a cozy horse-drawn sleigh ride
in Stockbridge, Massachusetts.
PHOTO BY JAMES KIRKIKIS/SHUTTERSTOCK

I love this picture because the snowflakes
look huge. They were even larger in person.
It felt like a snowstorm of snowballs.
KAYLA WULF *Owanka, South Dakota*

My daughter, Addy, is a true country girl
who loves animals. In winter, she and our
dogs are always eager to get out the sled.
SHERRY PEDERSON *Homer, Alaska*

I took this picture of my kids (from left), Rylan, Caleb and Piper, for our Christmas card. My husband, Stewart, bought this 1955 Chevrolet 3100 truck years ago with hopes of restoring it one day with the kids.
NICOLE FRASCHT *Mason City, Iowa*

My son Crewe was not a fan of snow, so he and his grandpa sat on the John Deere 5525 tractor and watched us sled.
SARA WHITE *Gilbert, Arizona*

A black-capped chickadee visited a festive basket that I made last winter.
RESPAH MITCHELL *Exeter, Maine*

This scene in Leavenworth, Washington, is from the Bavarian-themed
community's holiday lights festival.
PHOTO BY DANITA DELIMONT/ALAMY STOCK PHOTO

Hidden beneath the snow is my late grandfather's Ford 8N. This is our farm's original tractor, purchased in 1953, and five generations of family members have driven it.
ERIC SCHARTNER *Bolton, Massachusetts*

I came upon this barred owl during a chilly afternoon hike in Pinckney, Michigan. The owl was at peace.
LAURA KELLEY *Southfield, Michigan*

Our youngest son, Payton, was so excited to help bring the Christmas tree up to the house.
TRISHA GOETTLE *Avon, Montana*

We've adopted Keegan (left) and Christopher, and will soon add little brother Cooper. This was the first Christmas we all knew we'd be together forever, and they couldn't wait to choose a tree.
CHERYL STORK *Jonesborough, Tennessee*

HEART & SOUL

Dashing Through the Corn

A vintage tractor stands in for a sleigh on a moonlit ride to remember.

BY BARBARA WEDDLE *Oconto, Wisconsin*

My cousin Gilbert brought back to life a 1957 D17 Allis-Chalmers tractor. It had been faded by the sun and was dilapidated after languishing for years in the machine shed. But it now boasted a new coat of Persian Orange paint and an overhauled engine. The relic stood ready for a test run in the cornfield on Christmas Eve.

I was the last person to abandon the warmth of Gilbert's farmhouse to join in the fun. Excited voices greeted me as I took a seat on the trailer hitched behind the tractor.

When I was settled in, Gilbert put the tractor into gear. The trailer lurched as we bounced across the field. The temperature dipped to 5 below.

Gilbert coaxed the tractor down a slope onto a rutted dirt road, then steered it in the direction of the woods. A few dried corn leaves made ghostly apparitions under the soft glow of the moon. Light shone from one of the farmhouse windows like a star.

Someone whispered, "There's the Big Dipper."

We followed the road toward a stand of trees, went on through, and then bounced out into a clearing. Gilbert's son, Todd, began to sing "Away in a Manger." Soon everyone was caroling, our voices swelling to fill the air. We continued with "Hark! The Herald Angels Sing" and "The First Noel."

In the end it was not the tractor that failed us, but the trailer. Todd, realizing one of the tires had gone flat, yelled for Gilbert to halt.

I stared in awe at the stars above me. Thoughts of a Christmas Eve more than 50 years past came to mind—when my father, his voice merry with the trickiness of his claim, summoned his children to witness Santa's flight across a starry sky. This ride had ended too quickly. But I'll have another memory. ☀

Snowy farm fields were the perfect setting for an unforgettable winter night.

Richest Family in Town

*When her parents were in trouble at Christmas,
friendship taught her the true value of kindness.*

BY NINA SCHEPKER *Linn, Missouri*

I grew up on a 50-acre farm in the small rural community of Catawissa, Missouri, as the sixth of seven children. My parents often noted during meals how everything on the table except the sugar and flour came from the land.

Besides running the farm, Dad was also a carpenter. In the fall of 1970, he was working on a house when the ladder broke. His back was fractured in two places.

He stayed in the hospital for three weeks with his head and feet down, permitting his back to align correctly so the bones would fuse.

On Thanksgiving, Dad was still in the hospital. We always butchered hogs the day after the holiday, and that year my uncle showed up with a couple of cousins to help my three older brothers prepare our year's supply of pork.

After Dad returned home, he was in a back brace and unable to work or run the farm. I was too young to realize our family had no money coming in as Christmas approached.

One night we heard a car coming up the long driveway. Always alert to company, we kids were curious about who was visiting.

Peggy Phelan was at the door, holding an envelope stuffed with money. She told my dad she had collected money in the community and was there to deliver it.

He tried to protest but Peggy would have none of it. I can still hear her saying, "Archie, whenever someone's baler is broke, you bale their hay. Someone passes away, Altha is cooking. It's our turn."

That evening, this 6-year-old understood what being a good neighbor was, and that because her parents were good neighbors, their kindness was returned.

I learned later that my mom's sisters all "adopted" one of us kids to help with Christmas, and we received gift baskets from more than one organization.

My parents were used to being the givers and not the receivers of such generosity. They had a bit of pride to swallow, but continued all of their lives to show us kids the value of kindness. ☼

Caring angels repaid her parents' generosity by helping out on the farm.

Dottie, Robin and Shirley (from left) made baking day a tradition.

Ready, Set, Decorate!

A dusting of sugar and sprinkles turns time in the kitchen with family into sweet Christmas memories.

BY SHIRLEY BARBERIC *Grand Island, New York*

Baking Christmas cookies with my mom, Dottie, and my sister, Robin, is always a day filled with laughter, fun, memories of Christmas and lots of eggnog.

When we started our baking day tradition back in 1993, it was at my house. I was so excited to have Mom and Robin come over to make cookies. We baked all day, frosted all night and must have had at least six different kinds of cookies going at once: chocolate chip, Russian tea cakes, peanut butter, coconut macaroons, gingersnaps, strawberry thumbprints and, of course, the classic sugar cookie cutouts.

Robin and I had just started our families, and Mom was never one for the kitchen. So we really didn't know what we were doing. By the end of the day, we were exhausted and the kitchen was a disaster. But over the years we've refined our skills, and we're a little more organized. It's a lot of work, but we always have fun.

When our kids were little they helped us with the frosting, and maybe the cookies didn't always look bakery-perfect but they got eaten just the same. Older now, the kids come and go, but they still look for their favorites at the end of the day. I'd love to see them carry on this tradition. Until then I'm happy to bake for them.

Looking back over the years, I realize that those cookies are a lot like life. Sometimes they turn out great, but sometimes the cookies are a little burnt and rough around the edges. It's not really the cookies that make the season special. It's the people we bake with and for who make it all worthwhile. ☀

A Belated Christmas Gift

After almost 40 years, a family tractor shines anew.

BY PAUL WEST *Wichita, Kansas*

On the day after Christmas in 2014, I pulled this Farmall H out of the family barn where it had been sitting unused since 1976. My father, Lloyd, had bought the tractor from my grandfather John back in 1952, and then I bought it from my father in 1981.

Grandpa had purchased the H in 1941 from an International Harvester Co. dealer in La Crosse, Kansas, driving it 12 miles home to his farm near the small town of Nekoma.

My older brother remembers the tractor being used for fieldwork; I remember it pulling an irrigation pipe trailer and the hay wagons. In the winter, it was used to pull a feed wagon for cattle.

I had always intended to restore the tractor, but decades passed and I never got it done. Finally, on Dec. 26, 2014, I hired a helper, Cain Hyner, and we started the project. We discovered that mud dauber wasps had built nests on top of the engine's cylinders, rendering it immobile. We ground the engine down, removed all the sheet metal, sandblasted the entire tractor, and gave it an all-over undercoat of automobile paint, which lasts longer than machinery paint.

The H still features its original belt pulley. Cain and I upgraded the old 6-volt generator to a 12-volt system, making a dramatic difference in how the tractor starts.

All told, I spent more than $5,000 on the restoration. By comparison, Grandpa had bought the tractor new for around $1,100.

Farmall H tractors are not rare; you could find them on at least half the neighboring farms when I was growing up. But this particular H has been in my family for more than 75 years, and that makes it extremely special to me. ☀

Paul West's restored Farmall H is a treasured family heirloom.

To Grandmother's House We Sew

A grandma and granddaughter fused together a quilting legacy and a special bond with each other.

BY ELIZABETH BUSCH *Brookfield, Wisconsin*

When I was 7 years old, I simply loved spending the night at my Grandma Cecilia's house. My two sisters and I were fascinated with her sewing room. Our eyes lit up as we gazed in awe at the various baskets that held countless fabric pieces in every possible pattern.

At the time, we were too small to handle the power of the sewing machine, so we admired the baby blankets, quilts, dresses, pajama pants and pillowcases that my grandma made for us. As we got older, we each picked a project to work on every time we slept over. My first project began with close supervision from my grandma. We sat in the same chair, and she controlled the sewing machine pedal while I gently moved the fabric from side to side and back and forth.

Soon I was a sewing fanatic, fabricating pillowcase after pillowcase and giving them to any relative or friend who was interested. I customized each one according to the recipient, with designs like elaborate princess themes as well as simple and elegant versions.

But I could only put so much creativity into making pillowcases before this project became repetitive and dull. So my grandma urged me to try quilting. Having seen the many quilts she had made, I was familiar with the variety of styles and designs that could be incorporated into one piece. It was rather intimidating, knowing I had to think of a quilt design to pursue. But with a little help and inspiration from her, I got to work on my first wall quilt.

My grandma entered me into my first quilting competition, the 2009 Racine Quilt Show, when I was 10 years old. After months of dedicated preparation and long hours adhering to my grandma's quilting advice, it was rewarding to walk into the show with her and see a first-place blue ribbon pinned to my quilt. It depicted Snoople, my purple, octopus-like imaginary friend. My grandma snapped pictures and told all of her quilting friends. Happy to see a young face in the competition, they complimented me. I felt like a celebrity. I could tell how proud my grandma was, which made me feel satisfied knowing that I was upholding her sewing legacy. In that moment, I knew my sewing career had just begun.

During the summer of 2015, I entered the Racine Quilt Show again. I had about five months to complete my masterpiece. My grandma and I researched topics and patterns, and finally settled on a concept that we thought would look cute: I portrayed five different-colored whales atop a sea-blue background. Armed with the design that I'd sketched onto a piece of paper, I went to the fabric store with my grandma, and I chose cloth (although it was hard to stay focused among the wealth of colors and patterns).

I returned to my grandma's house with a mind full of ideas for the future, and I promptly started measuring, cutting, ironing, sewing and stitching my way to the finish. I spent countless hours in her sewing room leading up to that competition.

My completed quilt received a first-place award at the show. I was thrilled. More experienced competitors shook my hand and congratulated me on my hard-earned success.

The memories I hold closest, though, are not the blue ribbons or the cash prizes, but rather the bond my grandma and I have formed. I have stitched together skills and life lessons by quilting with her. Honestly, the reason I enjoy quilting so much is because it allows me to spend one-on-one time with her. I am lucky to have someone in my life who cares about me so much; becoming a quilter is an ode to my grandma and all she has done for me. ☀

Elizabeth wrote a version of this essay for her college applications, and many schools sent back acceptance letters. She now attends DePauw University in Greencastle, Indiana.

Cecilia Johnson helped granddaughter Elizabeth Busch become an award-winning quilter.

Checking Off His To-Do List

When Teddy the world traveler visits Grandpa's farm, tractor riding is a must.

BY ALISHA GRUBER *Bonaire, Georgia*

My 6-year-old son, Teddy, has done a lot of traveling. As a military kid, he visited 20 states before he turned 1, and he has lived in four different places, including Japan, in his first six years of life. Of all the places Teddy has been, his favorite is my family's farm in rural Iowa. He loves helping my dad, Ted, with his many farm chores, and the two enjoy spending entire days outside together. Last year, leading up to our visit at Grandpa Ted's, Teddy wrote out a to-do list of things he wanted to accomplish on the farm. The list included feeding the cows, driving Grandpa's tractor, riding horses, riding in the truck, feeding the kittens, eating Cheez Whiz and pulling trailers. Grandpa made sure Teddy completed his list and he even added an additional task. Grandpa saved his manure hauling until Teddy visited so he could have a buddy to ride along with him in the tractor. ☀

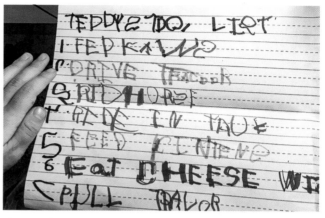

There's always so much to do when Teddy visits his grandfather's farm in Iowa. Grandpa Ted and Teddy are dressed for a full day of farm chores.

A piece of history is now hidden beneath newer layers of concrete in Linda Bailey's childhood barn.

Secret of the Feedway

*The family barn was the place to play,
and full of intrigue.*

BY LINDA BAILEY *Willow Hill, Illinois*

Some of my favorite memories were made in the barn on the century farm where I grew up. I loved finding kittens, new colts, calves—and sometimes puppies in the haymow. But roller-skating in the feedway was the best of all.

During World War II, my aunt bought me a pair of used skates, but because our sidewalks were made of rocks, I thought I had nowhere to use them. My dad said if I cleaned the barn's feedway, I could skate there.

When the feedway was swept clean, I discovered Burl Ives' name etched into the concrete. Burl had

been famous for some time, so I was quite surprised. But it turned out that Burl had been born less than a mile up the road from our barn, and he'd attended school with my dad.

Burl's dad was one of the first concrete contractors in the area, and Burl, at age 13, hauled sand from a nearby creek to the site where workers were mixing concrete for our barn. After it was poured, he wrote his name in our wet concrete. I spent many hours skating in that barn, listening to country music on the radio as I glided over Burl's name. ☀

Amish Chicken Corn Soup

PREP: 15 min. • **COOK:** 50 min.
MAKES: 12 servings (about 4 qt.)

1	medium onion, chopped
2	celery ribs, chopped
1	cup shredded carrots
2	lbs. boneless skinless chicken breasts, cubed
3	chicken bouillon cubes
1	tsp. salt
¼	tsp. pepper
12	cups water
2	cups uncooked egg noodles
2	cans (14¾ oz. each) cream-style corn
¼	cup butter

1. Place first eight ingredients in a Dutch oven; bring slowly to a boil. Reduce heat; simmer, uncovered, until chicken is no longer pink and vegetables are tender, about 30 minutes.

2. Stir in noodles, corn and butter. Cook, uncovered, until the noodles are tender, about 10 minutes, stirring occasionally.

1⅓ cups: 201 cal., 6g fat (3g sat. fat), 57mg chol., 697mg sod., 19g carb. (3g sugars, 2g fiber), 18g pro.
Diabetic exchanges: 2 lean meat, 1 starch, 1 fat.

Gingerbread Kisses

PREP: 35 min. + chilling • **BAKE:** 10 min./batch
MAKES: 5 dozen

- ¾ cup butter, softened
- ¾ cup packed brown sugar
- 1 large egg, room temperature
- ½ cup molasses
- 3 cups all-purpose flour
- 1 tsp. baking soda
- ¼ tsp. salt
- 2 tsp. ground ginger
- 1 tsp. ground cinnamon
- ¼ tsp. ground nutmeg
- ¼ cup sugar
- 60 striped chocolate kisses, unwrapped

1. Cream butter and brown sugar until light and fluffy. Gradually beat in egg and molasses. In another bowl, whisk together flour, baking soda, salt and spices; gradually beat into creamed mixture. Refrigerate, covered, until firm enough to shape, about 4 hours.
2. Preheat oven to 350°. Shape dough into sixty 1-in. balls; roll in sugar. Place 1 in. apart on ungreased baking sheets. Bake until lightly browned, 8-10 minutes.
3. Press a chocolate kiss immediately into the center of each cookie. Remove from pans to wire racks to cool.

1 cookie: 88 cal., 4g fat (2g sat. fat), 10mg chol., 56mg sod., 13g carb. (8g sugars, 0 fiber), 1g pro.

Festive Apple Dip

TAKES: 20 min. • **MAKES:** 8 servings

- 1 pkg. (8 oz.) cream cheese, softened
- ½ cup creamy peanut butter
- ⅓ cup packed brown sugar
- 1 tsp. vanilla extract
- ½ cup miniature marshmallows
- 1 jar (11¾ oz.) hot fudge ice cream topping
- 2 Tbsp. chopped mixed nuts or peanuts
- 3 each medium red and green apples, cut into thin wedges
- 2 Tbsp. lemon juice

1. For dip, beat first four ingredients until smooth; stir in marshmallows. Spoon half of the mixture into a 3-cup bowl; top with half of the fudge topping. Repeat layers. Sprinkle with nuts.
2. To serve, toss apples with lemon juice. Serve with dip.

¼ cup dip with ¾ apple: 403 cal., 22g fat (9g sat. fat), 29mg chol., 218mg sod., 49g carb. (38g sugars, 3g fiber), 8g pro.

Maple Sticky Buns

PREP: 30 min. + chilling • **BAKE:** 25 min. • **MAKES:** 2½ dozen

2	pkg. (¼ oz. each) active dry yeast
2	cups warm water (110° to 115°)
¼	cup shortening
½	cup sugar
1	large egg, room temperature
2	tsp. salt
6 to 6½	cups all-purpose flour
6	Tbsp. butter, softened
¾	cup packed brown sugar
1	Tbsp. ground cinnamon
¾	cup chopped walnuts
1½	cups maple syrup
	Additional brown sugar

1. In a large bowl, dissolve yeast in water. Add shortening, sugar, egg, salt and 5 cups flour. Beat until smooth. Add enough remaining flour to form a soft dough. Cover and refrigerate overnight or up to 24 hours.

2. Punch dough down. Turn onto a floured surface; knead until smooth and elastic, 6-8 minutes, adding more flour if needed. Divide into thirds. Roll each portion of dough into a 16x10-in. rectangle.

3. On each rectangle, spread 2 Tbsp. butter; sprinkle each with ¼ cup brown sugar, 1 tsp. cinnamon and ¼ cup walnuts. Pour the syrup into three greased 9-in. round baking pans. Sprinkle with additional brown sugar.

4. Tightly roll up each rectangle, jelly-roll style, starting with a short side. Slice each roll into 10 pieces; place over syrup. Cover and let rise until doubled, about 30 minutes.

5. Preheat oven to 350°. Bake until golden brown, 25-30 minutes. Cool in pans 5 minutes; invert onto serving plates.

1 sticky bun: 224 cal., 6g fat (2g sat. fat), 13mg chol., 187mg sod., 39g carb. (19g sugars, 1g fiber), 4g pro.

Apricot Ham Steak

TAKES: 10 min. • **MAKES:** 4 servings

2	Tbsp. butter, divided
4	fully cooked boneless ham steaks (5 oz. each)
½	cup apricot preserves
1	Tbsp. cider vinegar
¼	tsp. ground ginger
	Dash salt

1. In a large skillet, heat 1 Tbsp. butter over medium heat. Cook ham on both sides until lightly browned and heated through. Remove from pan; keep warm.

2. Add 1 Tbsp. butter and remaining ingredients to pan; cook and stir over medium heat until blended and heated through. Serve over ham.

1 ham steak: 299 cal., 11g fat (5g sat. fat), 88mg chol., 1899mg sod., 26g carb. (17g sugars, 0 fiber), 26g pro.

Lemony Roasted Chicken & Potatoes

PREP: 20 min. • **BAKE:** 40 min.
MAKES: 4 servings

- 1½ **lbs. red potatoes (about 5 medium), cut into ¾-in. cubes**
- 1 **large onion, coarsely chopped**
- 1 **medium lemon, halved and sliced**
- 3 **Tbsp. olive oil, divided**
- 3 **garlic cloves, minced**
- 1¼ **tsp. salt, divided**
- 1 **tsp. dried rosemary, crushed, divided**
- 1 **tsp. pepper, divided**
- 4 **bone-in chicken thighs (about 1½ lbs.)**
- 4 **chicken drumsticks (about 1 lb.)**
- 1 **tsp. paprika**
- 6 **cups fresh baby spinach (about 5 oz.)**
  Lemon wedges, optional

1. Preheat oven to 425°. Place potatoes, onion and sliced lemon in a large bowl; toss with 2 Tbsp. oil, garlic and ½ tsp. each salt, rosemary and pepper. Spread evenly in a greased roasting pan. Roast on an upper oven rack for 20 minutes.

2. Meanwhile, toss chicken with paprika and the remaining salt, rosemary and pepper. In a large skillet, heat remaining oil over medium-high heat. Brown chicken in batches.

3. Place chicken over potato mixture. Roast until a thermometer inserted in chicken reads 170° and potatoes are tender, 15-20 minutes. Remove chicken from pan. Immediately add spinach to vegetables, stirring to wilt slightly. Serve with chicken and, if desired, lemon wedges.

1 serving: 589 cal., 31g fat (7g sat. fat), 128mg chol., 898mg sod., 35g carb. (4g sugars, 5g fiber), 42g pro.

Beef Filets with Portobello Sauce

TAKES: 20 min.
MAKES: 2 servings

- 2 **beef tenderloin steaks (4 oz. each)**
- 1¾ **cups sliced baby portobello mushrooms (about 4 oz.)**
- ½ **cup dry red wine or reduced-sodium beef broth**
- 1 **tsp. all-purpose flour**
- ½ **cup reduced-sodium beef broth**
- 1 **tsp. ketchup**
- 1 **tsp. steak sauce**
- 1 **tsp. Worcestershire sauce**
- ½ **tsp. ground mustard**
- ¼ **tsp. pepper**
- ⅛ **tsp. salt**
- 1 **Tbsp. minced fresh chives, optional**

1. Place a large skillet coated with cooking spray over medium-high heat; brown steaks on both sides. Remove from pan.

2. Add mushrooms and wine to pan; bring to a boil over medium heat, stirring to loosen browned bits from pan. Cook until liquid is reduced by half, 2-3 minutes. Mix flour and broth until smooth; stir into pan. Stir in all remaining ingredients except chives; bring to a boil.

3. Return steaks to pan; cook, uncovered, until meat reaches desired doneness (for medium-rare, a thermometer should read 135°; medium, 140°), 1-2 minutes per side. If desired, sprinkle with chives.

1 serving: 247 cal., 7g fat (3g sat. fat), 51mg chol., 369mg sod., 7g carb. (3g sugars, 1g fiber), 27g pro.
Diabetic exchanges: 3 lean meat, 1 vegetable.

Goat Cheese Mushrooms

TAKES: 30 min. • **MAKES:** 2 dozen

24	**baby portobello mushrooms (about 1 lb.), stems removed**
½	**cup crumbled goat cheese**
½	**cup chopped drained roasted sweet red peppers**
	Pepper to taste
4	**tsp. olive oil**
	Chopped fresh parsley

1. Preheat oven to 375°. Place mushroom caps in a greased 15x10x1-in. baking pan. Fill each with 1 tsp. cheese; top each with 1 tsp. red pepper. Sprinkle with pepper; drizzle with oil.
2. Bake until mushrooms are tender, 15-18 minutes. Sprinkle with parsley.

1 stuffed mushroom: 19 cal., 1g fat (0 sat. fat), 3mg chol., 31mg sod., 1g carb. (1g sugars, 0 fiber), 1g pro.

Pecan Cherry Bark

PREP: 25 min. + chilling • **COOK:** 10 min. + cooling
MAKES: about 4 lbs.

¼	**cup butter, cubed**
½	**cup packed brown sugar**
	Dash ground nutmeg
	Dash ground cinnamon
1¾	**cups chopped pecans**
1	**lb. dark chocolate candy coating, coarsely chopped**
3	**Tbsp. shortening, divided**
1	**lb. milk chocolate candy coating, coarsely chopped**
1	**lb. white candy coating, coarsely chopped**
1¾	**cups dried cherries or cranberries**

1. In a large skillet, melt butter over medium heat. Stir in brown sugar and spices; bring to a boil. Cook and stir until sugar is completely dissolved, about 3 minutes. Stir in pecans until coated. Spread onto foil to cool.
2. Line two 15x10x1-in. pans with parchment or waxed paper. In a microwave, melt dark chocolate candy coating and 1 Tbsp. shortening, stirring until smooth. Divide between prepared pans, spreading to desired thickness. Refrigerate just until set, but not firm.
3. In microwave, melt milk chocolate candy coating and 1 Tbsp. shortening, stirring to blend; spread over dark chocolate layer. Refrigerate until set, but not firm.
4. Repeat with white candy coating and remaining shortening; spread over top. Sprinkle with cherries and candied pecans, pressing to adhere. Refrigerate until firm. Break into pieces.

1 oz.: 165 cal., 10g fat (6g sat. fat), 2mg chol., 7mg sod., 20g carb. (18g sugars, 1g fiber), 1g pro.

HANDCRAFTED WITH LOVE

A Step Up from Tradition

An old ladder lifts the holiday tree to new heights.

WHAT YOU'LL NEED

- Ladder
- Twinkle lights
- Ornaments
- Tree topper
- Wood stain, optional
- Foam brush or rags, optional
- Scissors
- Clear fishing line

DIRECTIONS

1. If desired, use foam brush or rag to stain the ladder. Dry completely.
2. Wrap twinkle lights around legs of ladder.
3. Using scissors, cut varying lengths of clear fishing line, looping one end around the top and steps of the ladder. Tie ornaments to the other ends, allowing them to hang in the open space between the two sides of the ladder.
4. Secure a tree topper or an illuminated star on the top step and plug it into the end of the light strand.

Pine Cone Firestarters

Gather up a bundle of pine cones, do a little DIY magic, and then sit back and enjoy a colorful fire.

WHAT YOU'LL NEED
- Natural, dry pine cones
- Clear candle wax
- Candle dye colors
- Tall tin can
- Metal tongs
- Baking sheet
- Aluminum foil
- Flame color additives (optional):
  - 1 cup table salt (yellow flame)
  - 1 cup borax (yellow-green flame)
  - 1 cup salt substitute with potassium (violet flame) or
  - 1 cup Epsom salts (white flame)

DIRECTIONS
1. Pretreatment for coloring flames (optional): Fill a bucket with ½ gallon hot water. Mix in one additive. Soak the pine cones in solution for 8 hours. Remove; let cones dry until fully opened and then dip in wax as below.
2. Melt clear wax in a double boiler over low heat and mix in candle dye. Remove from heat; pour into tall tin can, leaving space near top. With tongs, dip each pine cone into the melted wax until completely covered, then place on foil-lined baking sheet to stand until wax sets.
3. To use, place a pine cone on kindling and light a single scale. If pine cones have been pretreated with additives, burn only one color at a time.

Old-Fashioned Flair

Bedazzled Christmas cookie disks become inspired ornaments.

WHAT YOU'LL NEED
- Cookie-press disks
- 250-grit sandpaper
- White vinegar
- Black paint
- Rag
- Hot glue gun
- Colorful beads
- Jump rings
- Colorful ribbon

DIRECTIONS
1. Age new disks by lightly sanding them with 250-grit sandpaper, and soaking them in white vinegar for 3-5 minutes to distress the metal.
2. Pat dry and, with a rag, rub a small dab of black paint onto each disk.
3. Hot-glue such embellishments as colorful beads.
4. Hot-glue a jump ring (made for jewelry crafting) to back of disk from which to hang beads. Connect beads to one another with additional jump rings.
5. Hot-glue a loop of ribbon to the top of each disk.

"I believe the world is incomprehensibly beautiful—an endless prospect of magic and wonder."
— ANSEL ADAMS

Horses graze at Cades Cove in Great Smoky Mountains National Park, Tennessee.
PHOTO BY PAT & CHUCK BLACKLEY